RIGHT COLLEGE, RIGHT PRICE

THE NEW SYSTEM FOR DISCOVERING THE BEST COLLEGE FIT AT THE BEST PRICE

FRANK PALMASANI

Published by Sourcebooks, Inc.
P.O. Box 4410, Naperville, Illinois 60567-4410
(630) 961-3900
Fax: (630) 961-2168
www.sourcebooks.com

CIP data is on file with the publisher.

Printed and bound in the United States of America.
VP 10 9 8 7 6 5 4 3 2 1

CONTENTS

Part 1

THE PROBLEM AND THE SOLUTION

Chapter 1
The Problem

The way we've been choosing and paying for college for so many years is now broken, leaving families in tough financial situations or with excessive debt. But I'm here to tell you that, even faced with soaring tuition, a poor economy, and limited financial assistance, every family *can* find a great college at the right price. We just need to use a better method.

So much has changed during my thirty-plus years of working with families on selecting and paying for college. I've always attempted to help them determine how they could provide their son or daughter with the resources to attain a college education—and do it without destroying their own financial lives.

In the early years, the solution was simple: just get families to file forms correctly. Later, it became more complicated: help families understand the details of the financial aid system so that they could better plan, prepare, and learn how to maximize benefits.

But now, in the midst of the student debt crisis and a system gone wrong, these options are simply not good enough for most families. A government financial-aid system that was once the backbone of opportunities for low- and middle-income families can no longer be relied upon to help families solve their problems.

This story is a perfect example of the situation in which many families are finding themselves today.

Jennifer* was a high school senior when she received an official award letter from her top-choice school, Indiana University in Bloomington. However, her award letter listed a net price for the college—what her family would have to pay for her to attend after loans and grants—that was $12,000 more per year than what her family could afford. It was April of her senior year, and Jennifer needed to make a final college decision by May 1. She and her parents had no idea what to do next.

Unfortunately, Jennifer's story is common today. Jennifer was a terrific student. Her ACT composite score was 31, and her high school grades were mostly As. But she wasn't given the right approach to make her college choice affordable.

Jennifer believed that she had followed the correct steps during her college search process. After all, she did what high school guidance counselors and college admissions officers told her to do. During her junior year, she and her parents used a well-known and respected college-search software program to help them choose potential colleges. Jennifer focused on colleges in the Midwest that had business programs. When she entered these variables into the program, it generated a list of 327 schools. Jennifer then narrowed down the number of colleges by focusing only on those with an enrollment of 20,000 or more students, because she wanted to go to a large school.

Jennifer wanted to attend a school with a strong business program, so she turned next to *U.S. News & World Report.* She learned that Indiana University, the University of Illinois, the University of Michigan, and the University of Wisconsin-Madison all had highly respected business programs.

After visiting with college admissions officers at each of these schools, spending time on their websites, and visiting their campuses in the summer between her junior and

*All examples within this book are inspired by my experiences as a counselor. Names have been changed to protect the privacy of the individuals involved.

senior years, Jennifer decided to apply to all four schools. Together, the college applications cost the family $260.

Jennifer's guidance counselor and the college admissions officers told Jennifer and her family not to worry about cost. Each college admissions officer suggested that financial aid was available to qualified students and that merit academic scholarships might also be available.

Jennifer's parents attended several financial aid sessions at her high school. They learned that, once they filed a financial aid document called the FAFSA, they would receive their Expected Family Contribution (EFC) number. Colleges would use this number to determine how much financial aid the family would receive. Jennifer's parents could use this number as a good indicator of how much money they would have to pay out of pocket for her to attend college. Jennifer's parents used a program called FAFSA4caster to learn their EFC, which was $12,457. While this amount was high, they believed it was manageable.

Jennifer and her family were also prepared if the net price of college was slightly higher than that EFC number. During the winter of her senior year, Jennifer searched for private scholarships in case additional money was needed. (She was able to obtain a $1,000 one-time scholarship from a local Rotary club.) Her parents also had saved about $6,500 for her college needs. Jennifer was thrilled when she received acceptance letters from all of the four colleges.

However, the shock came in April when the official financial-award letters arrived. None of the schools had a net price anywhere close to the $12,500 that Jennifer and her family had expected. The closest option was their state's flagship school, the University of Illinois at Urbana. This school did not offer Jennifer a merit scholarship, and Jennifer only qualified for federal Direct Loans. Thus the college's net price was $27,500—and this appeared to be her best financial option of the four.

Indiana University, Jennifer's top-choice college, offered her a merit scholarship. The award letter also indicated that Jennifer qualified for federal Direct Loans, but in the end, the net price was still higher than for the University of Illinois. The two other schools, the University of Michigan and the University of Wisconsin, had net prices that were even higher. So not only was University of Illinois not her first choice in schools, but as the most "affordable," it cost more than double what her family could afford.

Extremely disappointed, Jennifer and her family were left with two bad options. She could attend the local community college begrudgingly or she could overextend—borrow more than she should—and attend any of her four options.

Jennifer was a great student. She did everything she thought she was supposed to do to find the right college. But in the end, she found herself needing to either go to community college or take on excessive debt.

This is just one example of the many ways the college financial aid system isn't working for today's families. The good news is that there is a better way that will help you find a great college at the right price.

I've created Financial Fit™—a college search method that helps families find affordable college options—and used it as the basis for both this book and the Financial Fit software program on www .collegecountdown.com. With these resources, I hope to solve the college debt crisis for families. I believe that by working together— parents, students, counselors, and colleges—we can do just that.

I realized a couple of years ago that I had to focus on what I could control. I can't control how colleges make pricing decisions. I could complain about the rising costs of college tuition and fees being well beyond inflation, but the complaint would not change the reality. I could complain about the federal and state governments' inability to increase their support to match the rising college costs, but looking at the other challenges that those entities have, that complaint seems almost unwarranted.

What I did realize, though, was that we could change how we search for schools.

Financial Fit offers a solution. Using the tools and resources provided in this book and the software program, every family can find affordable college options. No family—that's right, *no* family—has to borrow excessive amounts of money so that their child can receive an undergraduate college degree.

I am confident that by using the Financial Fit method you will be able to replace the angst and anxiety that you have about college costs (as a parent) with a hope that you can provide your son or daughter with something that you definitely want them to have—and you can do it without destroying their financial lives or your own in the process.

In this chapter, we'll take a closer look at the issues affecting the college search and financial aid system today so that you can see just how we got where we are and understand some of the biggest myths and misconceptions about paying for college. One of the biggest issues is the current college-search timeline.

The Traditional Timeline

The college search process was much simpler in the past. Years ago, most students considered only a few colleges, those that their friends planned to attend or perhaps those personally recommended by their guidance counselor. Paying for college was also easier back then. College was much more affordable twenty to thirty years ago than it is today. The requirements to receive financial aid were not as stringent, and at some schools, students could borrow enough money in student loans to cover the cost of tuition.

Today's high school students follow a completely different process in searching for a college. During their junior year, students begin to seriously think about which college they would like to attend. They attend college fairs and speak to college admissions counselors. And eventually, a counselor, parent, or friend introduces them to online college search programs.

With the click of a mouse, students can use these programs to access information about more than 2,000 four-year colleges and universities in the United States. To narrow down their search, they enter preferences such as whether they would like to attend a two-year or a four-year school, along with the desired location, school size, major, and extracurricular activities. (See Figure 1.1.)

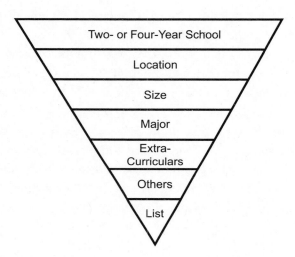

Figure 1.1: Traditional Factors Considered in Choosing a College

As the student enters preference after preference, the colleges that don't match up with these preferences are eliminated. Colleges that do match up stay on the list. The students can even get an idea of whether they will be accepted to these colleges by comparing their GPA and SAT/ACT scores with those of students who have been accepted and not accepted at these colleges.

Do you see anything missing so far in the factors students are considering in narrowing down their list of schools? That's right: price. Now, college search programs show each college's listed costs. But those costs are just the advertised price, what we call the "sticker price" (much like when you go to purchase a car). These programs are unable to compute how much students will receive from that college in grants, scholarships, and student loans, and thus how much that school will actually cost to attend (the "net price"). Without the ability to do this, the costs listed in college search programs have no meaning.

Once students and parents use college search software to create a list of potential colleges, they peruse these colleges' websites and perhaps visit some campuses. By the time the fall of senior year rolls around, many students are prepared to apply to six to ten schools. In most cases, these applications must be accompanied by an application fee that ranges from $30 to $90.

Even at that point, while students are applying to and being accepted by colleges, they have no idea how much each college will cost. College admissions and financial aid officers often do not help the situation. They may cite statistics that create the impression that many families receive financial aid from their school. Sometimes, they'll cite average aid awards to keep a family interested in their school.

Finally, in January of the students' senior year, the first step in finding out the real costs begins. Parents file the Free Application for Federal Student Aid (FAFSA). In some circumstances, parents must also file a CSS Profile, a supplemental form required by certain colleges. Financial aid officers use the results of these forms to construct financial-award letters.

In March or April of their senior year, students receive these official financial-award letters from the colleges that have accepted them. A typical award letter lists all grants, scholarships, student loans, and work options that a student will receive if he or she chooses to attend that particular college. After they analyze these award letters, families are finally able to determine the actual cost of colleges. They are finally able to see each school's "net price."

Now consider this typical scenario: A student, like Jennifer, has done exactly what she was told to do. She started the process by establishing an initial list of colleges. High school and admissions counselors encouraged her not to worry about the cost just yet. "Follow the timeline," they told her, "and everything will work out."

However, what happens when her official award letters arrive in March or April of her senior year and none of the colleges are affordable? And she only has until May 1 to decide what to do!

Disappointment sets in. Such disappointment usually leads the student and her family to pursue one of two options:

- **Option 1:** The student and her family decide that she should attend a local community college. Now, a community college is a great option when it's part of the original plan, but if a student decides to attend because he or she thinks there is no other option, the student may attend reluctantly and enter college without the enthusiasm needed for a successful first year.
- **Option 2:** The family decides to overextend its debt and chooses one of the unaffordable colleges. This option is much worse than the first. Parents often feel guilty if they don't overextend. They feel that their child has worked hard to get good grades and deserves to attend the college he or she wants. This thinking has created what the national media now calls the student debt crisis.

As you can see, the way we currently tell students how to search and apply for colleges leaves the major factor of costs completely out of the equation until too late. Fortunately, Financial Fit gives you a way to start seeing and planning for costs right from the start.

Ten Misconceptions about Paying for College

Another major problem with planning for college costs is the large amount of outdated or just plain incorrect information out there. This misinformation confuses parents and often leads to bad choices or missed opportunities. I've identified the top ten misconceptions about paying for college—and what the truth is—so you can avoid falling into any of these traps.

Misconception 1: College tuition today is so high and opportunities for help are so limited that only wealthy families can afford to send their kids to college.

Reality: Qualified students can attend college, regardless of their family's income, if they follow the right process and choose the right school. Sticker prices—what a school lists as its comprehensive costs—range from $2,500 per year at a community college to more than $55,000 per year at a highly selective private college. Families don't pay the sticker price, however. They pay the net price, which is the price after grants, scholarships, student loans, and work options are deducted. Some colleges offer impressive awards to lower their net price, which allow many students from lower- and middle-class households to attend college without accumulating excessive debt.

Yes, financial aid is more limited than it was in the past. States have tightened their budgets, and more students are applying to colleges than ever before. Qualifying for the Pell Grant, the largest source of federal financial aid, is also more difficult now. However, even if your son or daughter does not qualify for financial aid, he or she can still receive federal student loans, which are available to all full-time students regardless of income. There is an affordable college option for all families. The key is to learn how to find this option. The Financial Fit program will teach you how to do just that.

Misconception 2: The financial aid system supplies enough aid for all qualified students to attend the college of their choice.

Reality: The financial aid system is more limited than it was in the past. It *might* supply enough resources for qualified students to attend college—but not necessarily the college of their choice. Many students mistakenly believe that financial aid will allow them to attend any college. However, the process of matching what a family can afford with the net price of a school is the only way to ensure that a student can attend college without accumulating excessive debt. A family can't rely on the financial aid system alone to make that happen.

Misconception 3: The best colleges cost the most.

Reality: While elite colleges tend to come with higher sticker prices, as we've discussed, the sticker price is not what you pay. Many families find that their student's profile will result in some fantastic net prices at great schools. It's just a matter of determining that early in the process.

Also, recognize that there are no "best colleges." The best college for a student is one that fits the student in all ways. The student's academic profile matches the academic profile of the college. It has the student's desired major or program of study. It has the right "feel" for the student, so he or she feels comfortable there. More importantly, it is the best financial fit for the student. The student can attend the school without risking financial devastation after graduation.

Misconception 4: Your Expected Family Contribution (EFC) is what you must pay for your child to attend college.

Reality: EFC is one of the most misunderstood and misleading terms related to the college search process. Your EFC is calculated when you complete the FAFSA. The EFC is then used as part of this equation:

$$\text{Cost of Attendance} - \text{EFC} = \text{Need}$$

You'll read more about this in Chapter 9, "Understand Expected Family Contribution (EFC) and Its Relationship to Financial Aid." But basically, the EFC is just a number used to determine whether a student is eligible for certain financial aid programs. While financial aid officers at colleges need to know this number, it has little value to families because, at most schools, it does not translate into net price. In some cases, a family's net price is lower than its EFC, but in other cases, it's higher. Financial Fit will show you how to learn your *estimated* net price and your *official* net price at every school in the country. This is what will help you determine whether a college is affordable for your family.

Misconception 5: Students can borrow an unlimited amount of money to attend college.

Reality: Students can borrow a great deal of money to attend college—too much money, in some cases—but this amount is not unlimited. Every student can obtain federal Direct Loans, formerly called Stafford Loans, simply by filing the FAFSA. The Direct Loan program has a per-year maximum borrowing limit: Students may borrow $5,500 for their freshman year, $6,500 for their sophomore year, $7,500 for their junior year, and $7,500 for their senior year.

There are two types of Direct Loans: subsidized and unsubsidized. Both types are student loans and not parent loans. This means that they are written in the student's name, so the parent is not legally responsible to pay them. However, the terms of subsidized and unsubsidized loans are quite different. The subsidized Direct Loan is the more attractive of the two. No interest is accrued on a subsidized loan while the student is in college. The interest rate, which was 3.4 percent in 2012, does not begin to accrue until six months after graduation. The interest on an unsubsidized Direct Loan begins to accrue immediately, and the interest rate is higher. The interest rate on an unsubsidized Direct Loan was 6.8 percent in 2012.

Some students take the maximum amount of Direct Loans and acquire private student loans when more resources are needed. The private loans could have a higher interest rate. However, the goal of Financial Fit is to help you and your child avoid accumulating excessive debt.

Misconception 6: The key to getting financial aid is to learn how to "hide" your savings.

Reality: While the system that determines your family's eligibility for financial aid takes into account your family's income, it only takes into account certain assets, such as savings and investments. These are called reportable assets. Later in the book, you'll learn how these reportable assets impact the EFC number. Only in rare cases will repositioning of these assets lower a family's net price to attend a college. Sadly, though, some financial advisors recommend the repositioning of assets as a panacea and charge money for this recommendation even if the result doesn't impact the net price of college.

Misconception 7: If you don't claim your child on your tax return, your child can become independent and will receive more financial aid.

Reality: Your child is not considered independent simply because you didn't claim him or her on your tax return. Children can become independent, though, if they are wards of the court, homeless, in the military, or married. They are also considered independent if they have children whom they support financially. Students taking graduate courses and those who are twenty-four years old or older are also independent. If a student is deemed independent, the only financial information recorded on the FAFSA is the student's. Parents' financial information is not to be recorded.

Misconception 8: Students should find the college that most interests them before they begin searching for financial aid and scholarships.

Reality: Although a number of aspects of the Financial Fit program differ from other college-search methods, this one is the most critical. Students and parents following the Financial Fit program do *not* start the college search process by using college search programs, looking at college websites, visiting college campuses, and talking to college admissions officers. Instead, students and parents begin the college search process by systematically determining what they can actually afford to pay for college—and then looking for great colleges. This method is described in Chapter 2.

Misconception 9: Countless scholarship dollars remain unclaimed each year, but finding this money is difficult and time-consuming.

Reality: Thousands upon thousands of agencies and organizations offer private scholarships, but finding them is no longer difficult. Students can now use scholarship search databases to find relevant scholarships. Categorizing scholarships into these four groups and pursuing the groups in this order maximizes search results: workplace scholarships, local groups, regional groups, and national groups. We'll discuss finding and applying for scholarships in Chapter 11.

Misconception 10: If you make too much money, you shouldn't bother filing the FAFSA.

Reality: All families should file the FAFSA regardless of their income. Although the FAFSA determines your family's eligibility for need-based grants and subsidized student loans, other forms of aid are available regardless of your income and assets. If you want your child to have the opportunity to borrow some money to pay for college himself or herself, you need to file the FAFSA. You can't obtain Direct Loans unless you file this document.

Why Paying for College Is So Hard Today

While the issues with the timeline and many of the misconceptions about paying for college have been around for quite a while, paying for college today is much harder than even in the recent past. Several factors are driving this growing problem.

Soaring College Tuition

While the recession may have caused your family's wages to decrease, the cost of college has soared. Consider the increase from the 2001–2002 school year to the 2011–2012 one. The following average costs are according to the College Board and do not include room and board:

- Tuition and fees at a two-year public college increased from $1,748 to $3,122.
- Tuition and fees for in-state students at a four-year public college or university increased from $3,605 to $7,692.
- Tuition and fees at a four-year private college or university increased from $14,895 to $25,296.

Over the past ten years, the direct cost of college (tuition, fees, and room and board) at a private four-year college or university has increased an average of 5.4 percent per year. During this same time, the direct cost of college for an in-state student at a four-year public college or university has risen at an average rate of 6.2 percent.

During that same period, though, the average rate of inflation was only 2.26 percent, according to the U.S. Bureau of Labor Statistics.

These statistics have led to a new term, "college inflation." "College inflation" means that the costs of college are rising much more rapidly than the inflation of the economy as a whole, making college much less affordable for everyone. This would be a problem in any economy, but it is especially troublesome today.

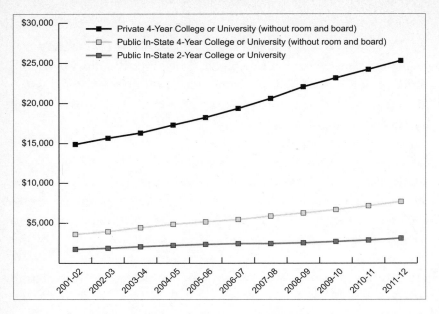

Figure 1.2: The Rising Cost of a College Education

A Poor Economy

Paying for college has never been easy, but it's more difficult now. The poor economy is partly to blame. The recent recession has left many people out of work. In 2010, the unemployment rate was a staggering 9.6 percent. It decreased in 2011, but by less than one percent. And in some states, such as California, Florida, and Michigan, the unemployment rate in 2011 remained higher than 10 percent.

If you are lucky enough to have a job today, you might not make as much money as you once did. The median household income in the United States has dipped from $51,295 in 1998 to $49,445 in 2011. (These incomes have been adjusted for inflation.)

The housing bust has also made it more difficult to borrow money for college. A decade ago, families had the option of borrowing against the value of their homes to fund a college education. Today, many families have lost the equity in their home, so their ability to use this equity as a borrowing source has decreased or been eliminated.

Limited Financial Assistance

As if the other problems weren't causing enough strain, the amount of financial assistance available to colleges is on the decline as well. The amount of money that states are willing to contribute to a public four-year college or university has decreased during the last decade, which means students have to pay higher tuition. In 2000, most states contributed more than $8,000 per student per year, and students paid $3,350 each. By 2010, most states contributed only $6,500 per student per year, and students had to pay $4,300. Why did states cut back on their funding? Many states feel their limited funds are needed elsewhere. Also, jobs are scarce and thus more students than ever are now enrolled in college.

A Perfect Storm

These are the realities. College costs have soared. The economy is challenging. Resources to families from states and the federal government have not kept up with college inflation. The result, of course, is that students and parents have borrowed significantly more money.

However, the method described in this book will help you personally avoid this problem of excessive debt. You'll learn what *not* to do, and more importantly, you'll learn what to do and when to do it. By following the recommendations provided, you'll ensure yourself an affordable college option and avoid excessive debt.

THE IMPACT OF PARENTS' FINANCIAL MISTAKES

After one of my seminars during the winter of 2008, a family called asking for a personal consultation. Laura was an assistant principal at a junior high school. She and her husband had a combined income of $150,000 and were raising four children. Two of their children were in high school. Like most families that attend my seminars, Laura and her husband wanted the very best for their children.

However, Laura was living in a sea of red. She had no equity left on her home after a first and second mortgage. The family owned two relatively new cars and had to make loan payments on them for another three to four years. Because of their income, they had little opportunity for need-based grants. Yet despite that good income, Laura had no discretionary income left each month and very little in savings.

Here was the kicker: At the age of forty, she was still paying off $70,000 of her own student-loan debt! Her monthly payment on that debt was more than $700.

The only college option for Laura's children was a two-year community college. After this, they could attempt to enter the workforce and accumulate enough savings to continue their education as working young adults and slowly complete their bachelor's degrees.

Laura's own college choice was her first poor financial decision. When I asked her how it all happened, she said, "During my senior year of high school, I was a pretty good student, but I came from a home where neither parent attended college. Everyone was encouraging me to find the best college possible. My parents wanted to give me the best, and my high school counselor encouraged me to pursue schools that fit me academically.

"I never even thought about cost because all the responsible adults told me that financial aid would be available. We filed the FAFSA and I received the grants they said I would receive. My parents had absolutely no resources and very little income. Sure, I was able to attain federal and state grant money, but it did not cover the high cost of attending my top-choice college. I had to borrow the rest. The financial aid officer at the college helped me attain a private loan beyond the Stafford, and I graduated with $50,000 of undergraduate debt.

"Although I started working soon after college, I needed a master's degree to advance myself. I kept deferring payment on the undergraduate debt as long as I could while incurring more debt to take graduate courses."

I asked Laura the obvious question: "Why did you attend the college you did when there were less expensive options available to you?"

Her answer helped me realize why Financial Fit is so important. She replied, "I didn't know any better. No one counseled me. No one stopped me, and responsible adults like my high school counselor and the college admissions counselor encouraged me to strive for the best college possible."

Laura's experience is not uncommon. So many families from the mid-1990s to the mid-2000s continued to purchase things they couldn't afford. They bought houses, cars, and educational opportunities by borrowing money—and now they and their children must suffer the consequences.

The Student Debt Crisis

The problems with the college cost system have gotten so large and widespread that this mounting debt is now referred to as a national crisis.

Too many college students today owe an extraordinary amount of money in student loans. They are borrowing twice the amount that they borrowed a decade ago (after adjusting for inflation).

In 2010, student borrowing surpassed $1 trillion for the first time. The Federal Reserve Bank of New York and other sources report that Americans now have more student-loan debt than credit-card debt. The average student debt is now approximately $25,000, and the average parent debt to help a child attend college is $34,000. Very soon, the average family debt to pay for college will surpass $60,000. Unlike other types of loans, student loans can be quite punishing. Even if students declare bankruptcy, they are still responsible for student loans.

We see the stories around us every day:

- A 26-year-old graduate from New York University who was attempting to manage a student debt of $100,000, as featured in an article by Ron Lieber in the May 28, 2010 edition of the *New York Times*.
- A 2009 graduate of Northeastern University who was carrying a $200,000 student debt load and was mentioned by writer Laura Rowley in a December 6, 2010 article on Yahoo! Finance.
- A student who accumulated $74,000 in student debt to pay for a business degree from Kent State University that Sue Shellenburger wrote about in "To Pay Off Loans, Grads Put Off Marriage, Children," published in the *Wall Street Journal* on April 18, 2012. Sixty percent of the student's monthly take-home pay is used to pay her monthly student-loan payment. Forty percent of her fiancé's paycheck is used to pay his monthly student-loan payment.

Clearly, the student debt crisis has long-term implications for everyone. You and your child can avoid this situation by choosing a college that you can afford. You'll start learning how to do this in the next chapter, "Overview of Financial Fit."

THERE ARE NO "SILVER BULLETS"

When I tell families that they need to begin the college search process by weeding out colleges that they cannot afford, they are not pleased. My message is not one that they want to hear. They do not want to hear that their child cannot go to his or her top-choice school because they, as a family, cannot afford this school.

Instead, they want me to show them how to find a scholarship that will cover the cost of the tuition at this school or tell them how they can hide their money so they appear to be poor and receive the maximum amount in financial aid. These families want me to come up with a "silver bullet," a magical way to make it work out so that their child is not disappointed.

The Financial Fit program is a practical way for families to send their children to college without accumulating excessive debt—but this method in no way promises that they will be able to send each child to his or her top-choice school. There are no silver bullets. If you purchase a home or a car that you can't afford, you'll suffer the consequences of excessive borrowing. The same is true of college. The key is to find an affordable school that is a financial fit for your family. And you need to do this early in the process so your child does not waste time pursuing college options that are unaffordable.

KEY POINTS

- Students today use college search software programs to select college options by entering preferences such as major, location, and school size.
- Many of these students select college options without learning the net price of these colleges until very late in the college search process. They may be disappointed to learn in March or April of their senior year that none of the colleges they applied to is affordable.
- When students and their parents follow the Financial Fit program, they first learn what they can afford to spend on college and then investigate colleges that match that affordability.
- Paying for college today is even more difficult than it was in the past because of soaring college tuition, a poor economy, and limited financial assistance.
- Students today are borrowing twice as much in student loans as students did in the past. This has led to what media calls the "student debt crisis."

CHAPTER 2
OVERVIEW OF FINANCIAL FIT

There are many problems with the way most students and families search for colleges, as we've mentioned. Luckily, the Financial Fit program gives us a great solution. Using this book or the Financial Fit software program on www.collegecountown.com, your family will be able to:

1. Figure out exactly what you can afford to spend on college.
2. Find colleges that you can afford.
3. Compare the costs of your college options to narrow down your list.
4. Understand the financial aid process and how to maximize your benefits.
5. Learn how to pay for college, including student and parent loan options.
6. Choose the right college and avoid excessive debt.

These resources will walk you step by step through everything you need to do to follow the method and get the right college at the right price. First, though, I want to give you a quick overview of the Financial Fit process as it appears in both the book and the online program so that, as you work on the steps, you'll have a complete sense of how they all work together and the importance of each step along the way.

The Financial Fit method has two main parts: the Planning Phase and the Execution Phase.

Planning Phase

1. Assess what you can afford to spend on college (your affordability). (Chapter 3)
2. Discuss your affordability with your child. (Chapter 4)
3. Understand the Financial Fit college categories and how they will affect college cost. (Chapter 5)
4. Use net price calculators and the Category Comparison Table to pinpoint Financial Fit college categories that you can afford. (Chapter 6)
5. Consider whether you need to implement the community college or the commuting option, or both, to make college affordable for your family. (Chapter 7)
6. Narrow down your list of colleges. (Chapter 8)

Execution Phase

7. Understand the Expected Family Contribution (EFC) and financial aid. (Chapter 9)
8. Discover merit scholarships. (Chapter 10)
9. Locate private scholarships. (Chapter 11)
10. Complete the FAFSA and, depending upon the college, the CSS Profile. (Chapter 12)
11. Maximize your child's benefits. (Chapter 13)
12. Interpret and analyze official award letters. (Chapter 14)
13. Understand the ten loan options. (Chapter 15)
14. Choose the right college at the right price. (Chapter 16)

Let's look briefly at each of these steps.

1. Assess Your Affordability

The first step in the Financial Fit program is to determine how much your family can afford to spend on college each year. You can determine the maximum amount your family can afford to spend on college (your affordability threshold) using the worksheet in Chapter 3 or calculate it automatically with the Financial Fit program's College Affordability Calculator™ on www.collegecountdown.com. Both of these resources follow ten steps to calculating your affordability threshold:

1. Determine tax credit eligibility
2. Consider your cash flow
3. Discover reduced expenses
4. Calculate eliminated payments
5. Redirect savings
6. Utilize available savings
7. Consider retirement funds
8. Include other available funds
9. Add new expenses
10. Define loan amount

2. Discuss Your Affordability with Your Child

Talking with your child about affordability can be tough. A lot of families aren't comfortable talking about money. Or you may fear disappointing your child by raising the issue of money up front. But if you are going to make a great college choice that doesn't result in heavy debt, parent and child need to be on the same page about affordability from the start.

Getting your son or daughter to understand how much you can afford to spend on college becomes even more challenging because of college marketing. Be aware that some colleges rely heavily on marketing to attract students. Many use marketing professionals to determine how to best present themselves to students and parents. A college's website, taglines, programs of study, and campus design may all be determined by marketing professionals. As a result, a student can become heavily invested in a college he or she may not be able to afford.

You need to convince your child that it is important to choose a college that is affordable. Most students don't think cost is an important factor in choosing a college. To them, an important factor is the look of the residence hall, the equipment available in the fitness center, or the benefits of belonging to a fraternity, sorority, or club on campus. Students want to have a good time at college, and the college marketers know that. Your child will be bombarded with images of the college experience that have nothing to do with affordability.

As a parent, you need to guide your child to make a good financial decision in choosing a college. While it's fine to consider a college's programs of study, location, size, and extracurricular activities, your child must also be aware of your family's financial limitations. These limitations should not cause him or her to believe that the only way to attend college is to borrow excessive amounts of money—much more money than the maximum allowed in Direct Loans. Your child also needs to be aware of the mistakes made by other students who chose to borrow beyond the maximum amount allowed through Direct Loans.

We'll discuss additional ways to get your son or daughter on the same page with you about your family's finances in Chapter 4.

THE ECONOMICS OF YOUR COLLEGE CHOICE

I am a guidance counselor at Hinsdale South High School, a suburban public school in Darien, Illinois, with a diverse student population of about 1,800 students. Our graduates matriculate to four-year state-supported colleges in and out of Illinois and to private colleges ranging from Ivy League schools to local institutions where many students live at home. In addition, about 25 percent of our graduates attend a local community college.

A few years ago, I created a classroom lesson plan called "The Economics of Your College Choice." I asked the economics and consumer-economics teachers at my school if I could teach one period of their class. The goal of "The Economics of Your College Choice" was to help students understand that the process of selecting a college is the first economic decision they will make.

For many years, students believed that their role in the college search process was to find a college they would like to attend—and their parents' role was to pay for this college. During the class, I told students that this philosophy works only if they have parents who are wealthy enough to write a check to pay for college without the student having to borrow money.

While some blessed families are in this situation, most are not. In many cases, both students and parents are financially involved in the college decision. Students must often borrow money, which makes them involved, and parents are involved in multiple ways, which might also include borrowing money.

I told the students in my class that they, like most college students, might use the Direct Loan program, which allows all students to borrow $5,500 during their freshman year, $6,500 during their sophomore year, and $7,500 in their junior and senior years. I explained that they will see the Direct Loan option in their award letters from colleges. In some cases, this may be the only benefit colleges offer them.

If students take Direct Loans at the maximum amount they are offered, which is $27,000 over four years, they will have a monthly payment of about $300 per month for ten years when they graduate from college. Statistics show that some students borrow more than the maximum amount allowed in Direct Loans through private loans.

Research suggests that more than 30 percent of the student population is now borrowing well beyond this

$27,000. For many young people, having to pay back so much money is stressful and puts them in financial jeopardy—all because of poor economic decisions. Students with high monthly payments might have to put off buying a car or a home, and even marrying.

At this point in the classroom lesson, I showed them the many articles that have been written about individual students who have ruined their financial lives by taking on too much debt.

In my class I pointed out that a good economic decision means choosing a college that they could attend while accumulating only reasonable debt or no debt. I told them that, after college, they would need to balance their monthly loan payments with the costs of renting an apartment, purchasing a car, paying insurance on the car, and otherwise supporting themselves. Perhaps this can be done with monthly student-loan payments of $300 or less. However, loan amounts requiring monthly payments of $400, $500, or more per month can be quite dangerous.

I have given students the following information. Based on a 6 percent interest rate and a ten-year monthly repayment, the amount they will pay on student loans will look like this, depending on how much they borrow:

$30,000 = $333 per month
$40,000 = $444 per month
$50,000 = $555 per month
$60,000 = $666 per month (and so on)

These figures help students see how every increase in their college debt will reduce the amount of money they will have each month after college to pay for things like cable, a car, Internet, and every-thing else they might enjoy.

COLLEGE SEARCH TIP

Don't eliminate colleges because they don't show up in a magazine's rating service.

The United States is home to more than 2,000 four-year colleges. The best college for your son or daughter is the one that fits in all ways. The school has to fit academically and must feel right to your child. The school must also fit financially. If a college is listed in a magazine as "one of the best" in a certain area but doesn't fit your child in these three areas, it is likely a bad choice, no matter how good its ratings are.

3. Understand the Financial Fit College Categories

Financial Fit is significantly different from all other college-search programs. Traditional college-search programs focus on finding colleges that are similar to one another. But similar colleges produce similar net prices—and those prices may not be affordable for your family. When you follow the Financial Fit program, you initially examine colleges that are very different from each other. These colleges will have very different net prices. Some categories will likely be affordable for your family, while others may not be. The goal is to give you a sense early on of which types of colleges will give you affordable options.

The Financial Fit college categories are:

1. Flagship state schools (within your state)
2. Non-flagship state schools (within your state)
3. Flagship state schools (out of state)
4. Non-flagship state schools (out of state)

5. Highly selective private schools
6. Midsize private schools
7. Traditional private schools
8. Community college and/or commuting options

You can find a list of colleges for each category in the Appendix or search for schools using the Financial Fit College Search Tool in the Financial Fit online software. We'll take a closer look at each of these categories in Chapter 5.

4. Use Net Price Calculators and the Category Comparison Table

The cost to attend a college is often listed on the college's website in the section about financial aid. The official name for this cost is the *cost of attendance*, but we refer to it as the "sticker price" in this book.

All colleges are required to list their sticker price. However, a college's sticker price is not the amount of money that most students pay to attend the college. Because some students are able to obtain grants, scholarships, and campus jobs and all students are able to obtain Direct Loans, no one has to pay the sticker price to attend college. Therefore, don't panic when you see that a college has a high sticker price. Focus on its net price.

Net price has this official definition:

Cost of Attendance − Grants and Scholarships = Net Price

Net price also has this practical definition, which colleges sometimes present to students:

Cost of Attendance − Grants, Scholarships, Student Loans, and Campus Employment = Net Price

Financial Fit focuses on net price. You can use net price calculators to determine the estimated net price of a college. Each college now has a net price calculator on its website, usually in the admissions or financial aid section.

Before the invention of the net price calculator, families did not learn the net price of a college until March or April of their child's senior year when the official award letters arrived. Because of this, savvy parents encouraged their children to apply to many schools—six, eight, ten, or more—hoping that they could compare net prices upon receiving official award letters.

Some guidance counselors also encouraged this practice. The standard line was: "You don't know which schools will accept you, and you don't know what type of financial aid offers you will receive, so make sure that you have enough options to make a final decision."

Applying to so many schools was expensive and time-consuming. Although this method allowed families to analyze multiple awards, the comparative analysis did not occur until very late in the process. Another problem was that even though students applied to multiple schools, if they applied to schools in the same college category, the net prices of those schools tended to be quite similar.

This all changed in 2008 when the U.S. Department of Education informed colleges that they needed to include a net price calculator on their website by October 2011. This allowed families to get an idea of what a particular college would cost much earlier in the college search process.

Net price calculators were designed as planning tools, so you should use them as such. Although not perfect, each calculator should give you a decent estimate of what your net price will be at a college if your son or daughter chooses to attend.

Some net price calculators are more accurate and reliable than others. Typically, the calculators that require you to enter more exact financial information and include questions about your child's academic performance are the most reliable.

A category comparison table compares the net prices of colleges in different categories. You should create this chart during the Planning Phase and fill it in using the colleges' net price calculators. You can create a second category comparison table during the Execution Phase when your child receives official award letters from colleges.

If you choose a college in each category and use that college's net price calculator during the Planning Phase, you should be able to reasonably determine whether that school matches what you can afford. If you use a college's net price calculator and discover that a category of colleges appears to be beyond your affordability, test that category with a few more schools. If none of them fit you financially, and especially if they are well beyond your affordability, then don't spend more time researching schools in this college category. Eliminate this category from those that you plan to investigate.

We'll discuss category comparison tables in detail in Chapter 6. You can also complete your own category comparison table online and save your results using the Financial Fit program software.

5. Consider Commuting/Community College Options

What if the net prices of all the categories are too high? When you follow the Financial Fit program, you also consider the commuting option. You can significantly reduce the net price of college if your child lives at home and commutes to school each day.

Room and board is expensive, between $8,000 and $10,000 at most schools. (See Figure 7.1.) Understandably, commuting is more common than you might believe. About 86 percent of college and university students commute to school. While some of these students live in off-campus apartments, many of them live at home.

Like the commuting option, the community college option may be right for your child, especially if your family does not receive enough need-based grants or merit awards, or both, from the colleges in the other categories. Whenever the net price of other colleges is out of reach, a community college can be an excellent choice for the first two years. You'll learn more in Chapter 7.

6. Narrow Down Your List of Colleges

After you and your child determine which college categories are affordable, you're ready to choose four to six schools from these categories to apply to. Since many of the schools within these categories will be a financial fit for your family, your son or daughter should consider other factors in choosing these schools, such as whether a school is an academic fit and a "feel fit."

Schools that are an academic fit will have the major your child wants to pursue. Students who are admitted to these schools will have high school grades and national test scores that are similar to your child's. If a school has the right "feel fit," your child will feel comfortable there. The atmosphere at such a school will appeal to your child. For example, a small traditional private school with a nurturing atmosphere might be a better feel fit for your child than a large, public university. In Chapter 8, we'll discuss academic fit, feel fit, and other factors your child should consider in selecting schools.

7. Understand the EFC and Financial Aid

The Expected Family Contribution (EFC) is a number that is calculated when a family completes and files the FAFSA, a document created by the U.S. Department of Education. Historically, when a family learned their EFC number, they viewed it as what they would be expected to pay the college. Today, a greater disparity exists between the amount of money a student receives in financial aid and the amount of money the student needs to attend college. In many cases today, colleges do not have enough money to meet 100 percent of a student's need.

8. Discover Merit Scholarships

Many schools try to make their net price more affordable by offering students merit awards, which are also called merit scholarships, merit aid, and merit money. Merit awards are not based on financial need. They are awarded for academics, athletics, or special talents. The amount of money a student may receive in merit awards varies from student to student and from college to college. We'll cover this more fully in Chapter 10.

9. Locate Private Scholarships

Private scholarships are those not given by the government or a college or university. Businesses, agencies, organizations, and clubs offer such scholarships. Obtaining a private scholarship is one way to lower the cost of college. In Chapter 11, we discuss how to find and apply for these scholarships.

10. File the FAFSA and CSS Profile

On or after January 1 of your child's senior year of high school, you can file the FAFSA. When you complete the FAFSA, you answer questions about your income and assets (excluding retirement plans), your child's income and assets, the size of your household, and the number of children in your household attending college. Some colleges require you to complete a document called a CSS Profile in addition to the FAFSA. We'll discuss the FAFSA and CSS Profile in Chapter 12, and you can also find detailed worksheets in the Financial Fit program at www.collegecountdown.com.

The FAFSA is used to determine your Expected Family Contribution (EFC), a number that helps determine your child's eligibility for financial aid programs such as federal grants, state grants, college need-based awards, work-study jobs, and subsidized student loans. In general, the lower your family's EFC number, the greater your child's eligibility for these programs. We discuss the EFC and its relationship to financial aid in detail in Chapter 9.

NEED-BASED AWARDS VERSUS MERIT-BASED AWARDS

Your child's eligibility for need-based awards is determined when you file the FAFSA. The government uses the information on the FAFSA to calculate your family's Expected Family Contribution (EFC), which, as you learned, is not the amount you have to pay out of pocket for college. The EFC is a number used to determine eligibility for certain federal programs and, in some cases, state programs. These programs are resources that colleges use to lower their sticker price and eventually to create your net price.

Some colleges also award money based on need. Although this is not a guarantee, many colleges will award some need-based grant money when a family's EFC number is lower than the college's cost of attendance. Often, the colleges that provide the most generous need-based awards are those in the highly selective private schools category, such as the Ivy League schools.

Some colleges today do not use the EFC to determine financial need. These colleges require you to complete a supplemental form called the CSS Profile. These colleges might have special need-based incentive programs based on a family's income. If a family's income level is lower than a certain amount, the college will offer a particular package. For example, one of these colleges requires families to contribute only 10 percent of its income. This contribution becomes the college's net price.

Most merit-based awards, on the other hand, have nothing to do with your family's income.

Colleges offering merit-based awards often make outstanding offers based on your child's gifts and talents, which are most often academic and athletic in nature. However, some colleges do offer merit-based money for music, art, theater, dance, debate, and a host of other potential attractive attributes that colleges desire from students.

Historically, merit-based awards have come from traditional private colleges that were not the most highly selective, and this is still true. However, state-supported colleges—particularly those that are not the state's flagship school—also offer merit-based awards.

11. Maximize Your Child's Benefits

You can increase the odds that your child will be offered merit scholarships (award money offered by colleges) by maximizing his or her benefits. The key is to make colleges aware of your child's talents so you can convince them to work with you to lower your net price. As we discuss in Chapter 13, to maximize your child's benefits, help him or her create a resume and develop relationships with college admissions officers.

12. Interpret and Analyze Official Award Letters

In March or April of his or her senior year, your child will receive official award letters from each college he or she has applied to. A college lists its net price in its official award letter. Many colleges list their sticker price on their award letters and then deduct awards that your child has received to then display the net price.

Award letters are not always easy to interpret, however. Colleges do not use the same format to list the costs included in their sticker price and the awards they are offering. In Chapter 14, we'll teach you how to accurately analyze award letters, so you can see which college has the lowest net price.

13. Understand the Ten Loan Options

Even students who receive grants, scholarships, and other types of aid may need to obtain student loans to cover the remaining cost of college. Student loans are like any other type of loan. You or your child must pay back the money you borrow—and with interest. The lower the interest rate, the less expensive the student loan is.

These loan options can be confusing, and as a parent, you should help your child make the best decisions about borrowing money for college.

We'll look at ten types of loans in Chapter 15.

14. Choose the Right College for the Right Price

If you ask college admissions officers if they are willing to negotiate their net price, what do you think they will say? They will say no! Yet, some will work with you to find additional awards to make the net price of their school affordable. As we discuss in Chapter 16, if your child really wants to attend a school that is slightly above your affordability threshold, meet with college admissions officers a second time and show them the other award letters your child has received. Ask them if their school might have additional financial programs that you missed.

Financial Fit in Action

Now that you have an overview of how the method works, you can see how both this book and the online software program will help you to make college affordable. You can utilize one or both of these resources to complete the Financial Fit program—see the back inside cover of this book for information about purchasing the software program at a discount. Though this book provides worksheets and detailed information you need to complete each step of the process on your own, using both the online program and the book simultaneously will allow you to streamline your process with automatic calculations and search tools. Let's take a look at how one family used it in their college search process.

Together John and Jody Smith have an annual income of $90,000. They have two children: Adam, a high school junior, and Sarah, a high school sophomore. The Smiths have $20,000 in a savings account for emergencies. Both John and Jody have pension plans at work, so their primarily goal is to pay for college rather than save for retirement. Adam is a good student: his high school GPA is 3.6 and his ACT score is 26. The Smiths live in Illinois.

The Smiths followed the Financial Fit program, so before they began looking at colleges, they determined what they could afford to pay for college each year without placing themselves or their children in financial jeopardy.

First, the Smiths completed the affordability worksheet in Chapter 3 of this book, which takes into account educational tax credits, cash flow, available savings after an emergency fund, and reasonable borrowing. Using the College Affordability Calculator, the Smiths determined that they could afford to pay $15,000 per year for college.

Once they had determined this amount, John and Jody encouraged Adam to choose one college as a sample in each of the seven categories. They planned to consider the eighth category, the community college and commuting options, if they were unable to find financial fits in the other seven categories.

Adam chose these schools to test each of the seven categories:

- Flagship school (in state): University of Illinois
- Non-flagship school (in state): Northern Illinois University
- Flagship school (out of state): Purdue University
- Non-flagship school (out of state): University of Wisconsin–La Crosse
- Highly selective private school: Duke University

- Midsize private school: Marquette University
- Traditional private school: North Park University

Using each school's net price calculator, the Smiths learned that three categories of colleges appeared to be unaffordable and four appeared to be affordable.

Let's walk through the non-affordable categories first. (Remember, the Smith's affordability threshold was $15,000 per year.)

The net price calculator for the University of Illinois, the flagship school within their state, came up with a net price of $22,472. Since this is the only flagship school in the state, the Smiths eliminated this category.

Purdue University, the flagship school (out of state), had an estimated net price of $31,992. This category also appeared to be unaffordable, but John and Judy encouraged Adam to test two more schools in this category to be sure. Adam tried Ohio State and the University of Iowa. The estimated net prices at these schools came up similarly, confirming that this category was unaffordable.

The midsize private college category also appeared to be out of reach. Marquette University had a net price of $28,162. The Smiths also investigated Saint Louis University and Creighton University, but these also had net prices that were too high, so the Smiths also eliminated this category.

Therefore, Adam and his parents eliminated schools in the flagship school (in state), flagship school (out of state), and midsize private school categories from their search.

The Smiths then focused on college categories that appeared to be affordable. Surprisingly, they noticed that the schools with the highest sticker prices, those in the highly selective private school category, appeared to be very affordable. However, Adam realized that getting accepted at these schools would be challenging for him because of his ACT score, which was strong but not exceptional. For reasons other than affordability, Adam and his family eliminated schools in this college category.

This left them with three affordable college categories: the non-flagship school (in state) category, the non-flagship school (out of state) category, and the traditional private school category.

Right College, Right Price

Adam then considered his two major preferences: he wanted a school that was relatively close to home and that offered majors in history and secondary education. Since the Smiths were from Illinois, Adam decided to investigate schools in Illinois, Wisconsin, Indiana, Michigan, and Iowa.

Based on affordability and his preferences, Adam was easily able to narrow down his list of potential colleges to twenty. Adam was a junior in high school at this time. As he made his way through the college search process, he talked to college admissions officers, viewed college websites, and visited several colleges during the summer. In the fall, he applied to four schools on his list.

Adam and his family completed the Execution Phase of the Financial Fit program after January 1 of senior year. By following this method, Adam found the perfect college option by May 1 of his senior year. The college fit him in all ways, especially financially.

Let's consider what would have happened if the Smiths had not followed the Financial Fit program. Adam would have identified his preference and searched for schools with history and secondary education majors. In Adam's junior year, Adam and his parents might have attended a program sponsored by his school's guidance department. Guidance counselors would have shown them how to use college search software to compare Adam's academic profile and preferences with the profiles of a number of colleges. Adam would have used this program to develop a list of potential colleges. He might have narrowed down the number of colleges by selecting only those that were close to home.

Then the Smith family might have pursued colleges that they really couldn't afford, thinking that scholarships and financial aid would make them affordable.

Adam might have spent up to a year pursuing colleges that seemed to fit him academically but that did not fit financially. Having only unaffordable college options could have led his family to excessive borrowing.

By following the Financial Fit program, you too will avoid this trap and find the right college at the right price for the perfect fit.

KEY POINTS

- During the Planning Phase of the Financial Fit program, you will assess your affordability, communicate this affordability to your child, and learn to understand the different college categories. You'll also use net price calculators to determine the estimated net price of each college and record this information in a category comparison table, as well as considering community college or commuting options. Your child will then apply to four to six colleges.

- During the Execution Phase, you and your child will search for private scholarships; file the FAFSA and, depending on the school, also the CSS Profile; and maximize your child's benefits. In addition, you'll interpret and analyze official award letters, and use the award letters when speaking to college admissions officers. As the final step, you'll choose the right college at the right price.

- Colleges can be grouped into eight categories: flagship schools (in state); non-flagship schools (in state); flagship schools (out of state); non-flagship schools (out of state); highly selective private schools; midsize private schools; traditional private schools; and community college and/or commuting options.

- Each college has a net price calculator on its website that you can use to determine your estimated net price at that school.

- The Financial Fit program on www.college countdown.com and this book are great resources to help you find affordable college options. You can utilize one or both of these resources to help your family find the right college at the right price.

Part 2

THE PLANNING
PHASE

CHAPTER 3

ASSESS YOUR AFFORDABILITY

The first step in Financial Fit is to determine how much money your family can afford to spend on college—your affordability. You may ask, why is this the first step?

If you think about it, that question is a bit unusual. With any other purchase, you wouldn't hesitate to consider affordability first. If you planned to buy an expensive camera, a car, or a house, you'd figure out what you could afford to spend and then work within that budget. That brings us to the problem with the traditional college process—it feels just like every other major purchase we make, but a key piece is missing.

Just as you would read up on cars or homes you might want to buy, you read about colleges your child would like to attend, view their websites, and talk to college admissions officers. You narrow down your options and learn all you can about those options. You and your child might even take a few colleges for a "test drive" by visiting their campuses and talking to students who go there. In time, you and your son or daughter choose the college that you believe is the best fit.

However, at this point the process becomes different from other major purchases because the college then tells you and your child whether or not you may "purchase" it. If the college selects your child, you may now "buy" it. But even then, you still don't know how much the college costs! This is not determined until much later in the process.

Imagine if the sale of other goods or services was handled this way. A real estate agent could get you to fall in love with a house without telling you its price. The agent would not reveal this until the closing. An automobile salesperson would "sell" you a car and even let you drive it—but he wouldn't tell you the price of the car until you were ready to sign the papers to purchase it. It sounds absurd, doesn't it? Yet this is exactly what happens to many families when they follow the traditional process of choosing a college.

Financial Fit changes all that. When you follow this method, you first consider how much your family can pay for college and then choose colleges that are a financial fit. You learn the estimated net prices of colleges early on so your child will have multiple college options that you can afford.

Determine Your Affordability Threshold

You should begin to determine your affordability before or early in your child's junior year (but don't worry if you're getting a late start). To determine your affordability threshold, which is the maximum amount of money you have available to spend on college, use the Financial Fit software program's College Affordability Calculator or complete Worksheet 1 in this chapter. The worksheet is divided into ten steps:

1. Determine tax credit eligibility
2. Consider your cash flow
3. Discover reduced expenses
4. Calculate eliminated payments
5. Redirect savings
6. Utilize available savings
7. Consider retirement funds
8. Include other available funds
9. Add new expenses
10. Define loan amount

1. Determine Tax Credit Eligibility

The Tax Relief Act of 2008 established a very attractive tax-credit program for families paying for college. Families with an adjusted gross income (AGI) of less than $160,000 receive a full tax credit of $2,500 for each child attending college in the year that those college costs are paid. These college costs must be $4,000 per year or more. Note that a tax credit is a dollar-for-dollar reduction of the amount of federal taxes you must pay, so a family eligible for a $2,500 tax credit can use the $2,500 to pay for college.

Partial tax credits are also available for families with an AGI beyond $160,000 but less than $180,000. Note that a single-parent family has an income threshold of $80,000 or lower for the full tax credit and between $80,000 and $90,000 for the partial tax credit.

2. Consider Your Cash Flow

An important part of assessing your affordability is determining how much money you can spend per year on college out of your earnings. Itemize your bills. How much money is left after you make monthly payments on a mortgage payment, a car loan, and a credit card? What about after you pay utilities and household expenses? Most families don't account for every dollar they spend—some have no idea where their extra money goes. You might be surprised to discover that you have a few hundred dollars per month that you can use to pay for college out of your cash flow without changing your lifestyle at all.

Other cash-flow questions ask you to think about what you could sacrifice to help pay for college. Instead of buying breakfast on your way to work, you might bring it from home. How much money would this save per month? Maybe you could cut down on the money you spend going out to movies or skip a summer vacation. Most families realize that they have to make sacrifices to send their kids to college.

3. Discover Reduced Expenses

You may discover that some of your current expenses will be reduced or even eliminated when your child goes to college. Consider the current costs for your child's high school education. Do you pay tuition or fees? Will you be able to eliminate any expenses for extra-curricular activities including sports, clubs, or private lessons? You should also calculate how much your family will save on normal food and living expenses now that your son or daughter is out of the house and attending college. You will be able to direct these savings toward your child's college education.

4. Eliminate Payments

You may be able to increase your affordability threshold by eliminating some of your current payments before your child attends college. For example, if you are able to finish paying off a car loan or mortgage payments before your child leaves for school, that extra cash flow can be directed toward their college education. Similarly, if you are able to eliminate monthly charges on a credit card, those savings could also help to pay for college. Another option to consider is consolidating your loans—especially in today's low interest rate environment. Consolidating your debt and lowering interest rates may be able to free up some of your cash flow for college.

5. Redirect Savings

If you currently commit a percentage of your cash flow to savings every month, you may want to redirect some of those savings toward paying for college. Ask yourself if you have any savings that you would be able to suspend. If so, how much of those savings would you be able to direct towards paying for a college education? As long as this method does not interfere with your emergency savings, this can be a great option to increase your affordability threshold.

6. Utilize Available Savings

You may have accumulated money over time to pay for college, paying a certain amount each month into a fund. Remember, though, if you have been saving regularly for college, you can now take this monthly allotment into consideration when calculating your affordability threshold. You can also utilize the available savings that have accumulated with your 529 plan, pre-pay tuition plan, UTMA account, or any other vehicle that can be liquidated. Keep in mind that it is important to have money set aside for extraordinary circumstances. You do not want to tap into your emergency savings to raise your affordability threshold.

7. Consider Retirement Funds

Before you decide to utilize your retirement fund as a method to pay for college, there are a few questions you should ask yourself. When you retire, will you have little to no debt? When do you plan to retire and can you extend that period of time? Some families decide to postpone their retirement to come up with the resources they need to pay for college. This is a personal decision, and you should think about whether postponing retirement is something you would consider.

You should also take your other retirement vehicles into account, such as a defined benefit program or pension program, which might make taking money out of retirement or borrowing against your 401k easier. (Learn more about how you can use Roth IRAs or traditional IRAs to help you pay for college in the Financial Fit program at www.collegecountdown.com.) With these variables in mind, you may be able to take some money out of a retirement account and use it to pay for college.

8. Include Other Available Funds

Now is the time to consider any incoming funds that have not yet been included. This can be anything from the sale of your home or any large item to a planned monetary gift from a relative. If you are expecting unusual income such as a bonus or an inheritance before your child goes to college, this extra cash flow can be directed toward paying for their education.

9. Add New Expenses

Until this point, we have calculated the extra cash flow that we could utilize to raise your affordability threshold. On the flip side, you must calculate any expenses that your family will incur in addition to college costs. If you bought a new car recently, you will have to add your car loan into this calculation. You may have new expenses for another child, such as high school tuition fees, or maybe you intend to go back to school as well. These expenses will ultimately lower your college affordability threshold.

10. Define Loan Amount

Your child may obtain student loans to help pay for college. Federal student loans, called Direct Loans, are in your child's name. You are not responsible for repaying these loans. However, Direct Loans almost never cover the entire cost of college.

There is also a federal loan available to parents called the Parent Loan to Undergraduate Students or PLUS. We'll discuss the PLUS and other loans that can be used to help pay for college in Chapter 15, "Understand the Ten Loan Options."

YOU MAY HAVE MORE MONEY THAN YOU THINK

Frank and Joan Edmonson are the parents of two children, a high school junior and a seventh-grader. When they came to me, they were convinced that they did not have enough money to send their kids to college. They had heard the many horror stories about students who have accumulated excessive debt and did not want their children to go through this. They also felt guilty about their limited savings. While they had managed to save $20,000 for each child, this was not even enough to cover the direct costs of one year at their local state school.

I walked the Edmonsons through Worksheet 1 in this chapter. Since together they earned $110,000, they were eligible for the $2,500-per-year tax credit, which they weren't aware of. After answering the questions about cash flow, they realized that they had $500 per month ($6,000 per year) to use to pay for college. After a few more questions, they realized that they now had $8,500 per year to pay for college.

Next I told them to divide the $20,000 they had saved for the first child by four, assuming their child would attend college for four years. When they added this amount to the $8,500, they had $13,500 to pay for each year of college.

One of the Edmonsons had a pension program available through work, so they were willing to liquidate a $20,000 Roth IRA. This brought the total amount they could pay per year to $18,500.

The Edmonsons were now ready to discuss their financial situation with their child. If they were asked how much they had available to pay for college before our meeting, they might have said between $5,000 and $6,000. After they completed the worksheet, they realized that this figure was much higher.

The College Affordability Calculator makes the calculations automatically (visit Financial Fit program at www.collegecountdown.com for more information). You can also use the worksheet in this chapter and a calculator to make the calculations.

Worksheet 1: Affordability Worksheet

Financial Category/Step

Step 1—Determine Tax Credit Eligibility

For the year prior to your student begins college:

1. Conclude whether you will file your taxes singly or jointly.
2. Look to the correct table and choose one of the three categories to represent your household income.

Step 2—Consider Your Cash Flow

Considering your current cash flow, how much do you believe you could contribute to college costs directly—either from non-allocated income or lifestyle sacrifices?

For example:

- eating out less
- reduced entertainment expense
- use of public transportation
- excess cash not directed elsewhere

Step 3—Discover Reduced Expenses

Are there any expenses you have now for your college-bound child that you will not have when your child is in college?

For example:

- high school tuition or fees
- extracurricular expenses (sports, clubs, etc.)
- private lessons, summer camp, etc.
- food and living expenses

nount

Filing Singly		Filing Jointly	
Adjusted Gross Income	Tax Credit Eligibility	Adjusted Gross Income	Tax Credit Eligibility
?ss than $80,000	**$2,500**	Less than $160,000	**$2,500**
$80,000– $89,999.99	**$1,500**	$160,000– $179,999.99	**$1,500**
Greater than of ?qual to $90,000	**$0**	Greater than or equal to $180,000	**$0**

Description	Amount	# of Times Per Year

Description	Amount	# of Times Per Year

Worksheet 1: Affordability Worksheet, cont.

Financial Category/Step

Step 4—Calculate Eliminated Payments

Are there other payments that will be eliminated by the time your child starts college?

For example:

- credit card payments
- car loans
- mortgage payments
- other loans

Step 5—Redirect Savings

Is there an amount that you commit to savings every month that you could redirect while your child is in college to help cover college costs?

Step 6—Utilize Available Savings

After setting aside an amount designated for emergencies, are there savings available that can be used toward college costs?

For example:

- 529 plan
- pre-pay tuition plan
- UTMA account
- other vehicle that could be liquidated

Amount

Description	Amount	# of Times Per Year

Monthly amount that can be used toward college costs instead of being directed into savings:

_____ per month

Description	Amount

Worksheet 1: Affordability Worksheet, cont.

Step 7—Consider Retirement Funds

Without disrupting retirement, are there any retirement accounts from which you are willing and able to withdraw or borrow to help pay for college?

Step 8—Include Other Available Funds

Are there any other funds designated for college costs that have not yet been included?

For example:

- planned gift from a relative
- sale of home or other large item
- expected unusual income, such as a bonus or inheritance

Description	Amount

Description	Amount

Worksheet 1: Affordability Worksheet, cont.

Step 9—Add New Expenses

The flip side: Besides the college costs for your child, are there any additional expenses you will incur when your child starts college? For example:

- new car loan
- new expense for another child, such as H.S. tuition/fees
- new education expense for a parent

Step 10—Define Loan Amount

Using PLUS loan standards (fixed interest rate; 10-year repayment option; payments begin immediately), how much per month are you willing and able to pay in a loan payment for 10 years? This amount is in addition to the amount designated earlier out of "cash flow."

Examples (PLUS loans):

- Option A: $2,500 = $31 payment per month
- Option B: $5,000 = $61 payment per month
- Option C: $7,500 = $91 payment per month
- Option D: $10,000 = $121 payment per month

Description	Amount	# of Times Per Year

Monthly loan payment amount:

_____

Now that you've determined the top amount you can afford to pay each year for college, it's time to talk with your child and get everyone on the same page.

KEY POINTS

- The first step in the Financial Fit program is to assess your affordability. You can use Worksheet 1 in this chapter to do that. This worksheet and the College Affordability Calculator are available online at www.collegecountdown.com.
- Completing this worksheet will help you determine your affordability threshold, the maximum amount of money you can afford to spend on college.

CHAPTER 4

DISCUSS YOUR AFFORDABILITY WITH YOUR CHILD

The second step in Financial Fit is a difficult one—getting your son or daughter on the same page with you about what your family can afford to pay for college.

As we mentioned in Chapter 2, young people rarely consider finances in choosing a college. They might think that the cost of a college is less important than the size of its dorm rooms or fitness center.

In some families, talking about the family's finances is a regular occurrence. If this is the case with your family, this conversation with your child will likely be easier. But most of us rarely talk about money with our kids. It can be an uncomfortable topic to talk about: either we don't want them to worry or to feel like their options are restricted, or perhaps our parents never talked with us about money, either.

No matter what the case, having this conversation is very important. Don't skip this step! If your child is on the same page with you from the start about finding affordable colleges, you will avoid any of the confusion or hurt feelings that might lead later to bad decisions.

Explaining your family's finances to your child takes patience and persistence on your part. Every family is different in how this conversation is best handled, but here are some basic guidelines that should help any family.

Share Your Affordability Worksheet

Show your son or daughter the affordability threshold you determined by completing Worksheet 1. Stress the importance of having *multiple* college options that are in your affordability range. Your child should not get his or her heart set on one particular school because this school may not be affordable.

Discuss the College Categories

Go over the categories of schools with your child. (See Chapter 5.) You'll want to consider a college in each category so you can learn whether colleges in that category are affordable.

The key to the Financial Fit college categories is net price variety. You'll learn in the next chapter that the estimated net price of colleges varies from category to category. This is extremely important. It keeps you from wasting time and points you in the right direction—toward researching colleges that appear to be affordable and avoiding those that are not.

In the end, you may be able to group all college options into these three categories:

1. Schools that you can attend without accumulating any debt
2. Schools that you can attend and accumulate reasonable debt
3. Schools that you can attend only if you accumulate excessive debt

Teach Them about Loans

Familiarize your son or daughter with the Direct Loan program and the maximum amount that can be borrowed under this program: $5,500 for the freshman year, $6,500 for the sophomore year, $7,500 for the junior year, and $7,500 for the senior year. Explain that many students obtain Direct Loans for college. Tell your child that if he or she uses this program and borrows the maximum amount it allows, after graduation he or she will have a monthly payment of about $300 for ten years. As a family, you should determine whether this is a reasonable amount to borrow.

Point out that while most college graduates effectively manage a monthly payment of about $300 or less per month, payments higher than this often negatively affect their lifestyle. They might have to live at home longer than planned. They may have to delay buying a car, renting an apartment, and even getting married and starting a family. This is why we recommend that a student borrow no more than the maximum allowed in Direct Loans.

BE AWARE OF THE COLLEGE MARKETING MACHINE

Getting children on the same page with parents regarding the college selection process is no easy task. The college marketing machine is in large part to blame for this. Students are immersed in college marketing from the beginning of their junior year until May 1 of their senior year.

Colleges send mail and email encouraging students to visit their campuses. When students visit a college campus, they are exposed to additional marketing. In addition, some colleges have sports teams that frequently appear on television. All of that marketing can make a student choose a school without considering affordability.

I have talked to many parents who had trouble getting their child to understand their family's finances and why choosing an affordable college makes sense. In two-parent homes, one parent often is conscious of the family's finances while the other wants the child to attend his or her college of choice. In a divorced household, the situation is especially complex.

Mike called me to ask if I would speak with his ex-wife, Susan, and his daughter, Janet, about the colleges Janet was pursuing. Mike was Janet's non-custodial parent.

According to the divorce decree, Mike had to pay 33 percent of Janet's college costs. Susan and Janet each had to pay 33 percent. Dividing the cost of college is not uncommon in divorced households. Judges distribute assets and then make a decree regarding the legal responsibility for college costs.

Neither Mike nor Susan had any money to commit to college. They used the savings they once had to pay legal fees when they divorced. Although Janet was eligible for a substantial amount of need-based aid, her net price still varied from one college category to another. If she had looked, she would have been able to find affordable college options.

However, she became a victim of the college marketing machine early in the college search process. Janet set her sights on two midsize private colleges in large cities. She felt that she needed to get away and wanted to attend a well-known city school.

Susan stood by her daughter and wanted her to attend one of the two schools. She felt that this was just another issue she and Mike would argue about. Mike, on the other hand, wanted both Susan and Janet to understand that these schools cost much more than they could afford to pay.

I decided to first meet with Janet without Susan. "Janet," I said, "I know you have been pursuing these two colleges. They are excellent options. I know many students who have attended these schools. They have told me that they especially enjoyed campus life. I was wondering, though, if you wanted to consider some backup options in case neither school turns out to be affordable."

I then explained to Janet that she could group her college options into these categories:

- Colleges she could attend with no debt
- Colleges she could attend with reasonable debt
- Colleges she could attend with excessive debt

"The two schools you are considering fall into the excessive debt category, and that concerns me," I explained.

After discussing the long-term implications of a private loan as a supplement to the maximum amount allowed in Direct Loans, I convinced her that she should consider colleges in the reasonable debt category.

I didn't initially include Susan in that discussion because I was worried she would think that I was taking Mike's side. Yet, I couldn't in good conscience allow Janet to make a decision that would negatively impact her future. Once Janet started to see the benefit of this line of thinking, I contacted Susan and we had a similar conversation.

The situation turned out well. Janet is pleased with her college choice—and she chose a college that she could attend without accumulating excessive debt.

Show Them the Impact on Other Students

If you and your child are still not on the same page, show him or her articles about the student debt crisis and the negative impact too much debt has had on young people. Unfortunately, these articles can be found easily today online. A new one appears almost every day. Sometimes students have trouble seeing how a big–picture problem like finances affects them. Seeing the struggles that some of their peers are going through will help them see the importance of entering college the right, affordable way.

KEY POINTS

- You need to discuss your family's affordability and financial situation with your child. Don't skip this step.
- Show your affordability worksheet to your child and discuss your financial situation.
- Discuss the college categories covered in Chapter 5 to let them see a variety of options.
- Get your child on the same page with you regarding how much you can afford to spend on college by discussing loans and showing them the struggles of other students.

CHAPTER 5

UNDERSTAND THE FINANCIAL FIT COLLEGE CATEGORIES

Colleges tend to group into eight categories in terms of their price and affordability for different students.

As we mentioned earlier, similar colleges produce similar net prices—and those prices may not be affordable for your family. But by understanding all eight categories and testing out the net prices of colleges in each one, you'll get a sense of some very different net prices at very different colleges. Some categories will likely be affordable for your family, while others may not. The goal is to give you a sense early on of which types of colleges will give you affordable options so you can begin to narrow your search.

To refresh your memory, the Financial Fit college categories are:

1. Flagship state schools (in state, meaning they are located within your state)
2. Non-flagship state schools (in state)
3. Flagship state schools (out of state)
4. Non-flagship state schools (out of state)
5. Highly selective private schools
6. Midsize private schools
7. Traditional private schools
8. Community college and/or commuting options

THE FINANCIAL FIT COLLEGE CATEGORIES

To refresh your memory and for quick reference, the Financial Fit college categories are included here.

1. Flagship State Schools (within your state)
2. Non-Flagship State Schools (within your state)
3. Flagship State Schools (out of state)
4. Non-Flagship State Schools (out of state)
5. Highly Selective Private Schools
6. Midsize Private Schools
7. Traditional Private Schools
8. Community College and/or Commuting Options

Let's take a closer look at each category:

1. Flagship State Schools (In State)

A flagship state school is considered the premier public college or university within a state. Every state has a flagship school, and some states have more than one. A flagship state college or university typically has a greater enrollment and more stringent admission requirements than other state schools. A flagship school often participates in Division I athletics. For example, the flagship school in Wisconsin is the University of Wisconsin-Madison. The flagship schools in Michigan are the University of Michigan and Michigan State University. The flagship school in Missouri is the University of Missouri-Columbia.

State schools usually offer residents of their state lower tuition. For this reason, many students consider attending the flagship school within their state. Be aware, however, that these schools may not offer additional grants and scholarships to in-state residents that would further lower the schools' sticker price.

2. Non-Flagship State Schools (In State)

Every state has multiple non-flagship state schools. While some states have two or three of these schools, others have eight or more. A school gets classified in this category if it is state-supported but not the flagship school.

Non-flagship state schools may have fewer students and lower admission standards. Note, however, that many non-flagship schools have admissions standards similar to those of their state's flagship school. Don't misinterpret the term "non-flagship" as necessarily indicating a lesser-quality school.

Many families find non-flagship schools to be a financial fit, especially if these schools offer a significant tuition reduction for in-state students. However, non-flagship state schools within your state will most likely offer fewer grants and scholarships than traditional private schools.

ESTABLISHING IN-STATE RESIDENCY

In some cases, savvy families can minimize the out-of-state tuition disadvantage. A few years ago, a friend who is also a guidance counselor told me that all three of her children attended the University of Missouri-Columbia. Like me, she is a resident of Illinois. After one year at the college, each of her children was able to establish Missouri residency. The in-state tuition rate at the college then made the net price reasonable for her family.

Establishing in-state residency depends upon the requirements of the state and of that particular school. However, this may be an option in making a desired college a financial fit.

3. Flagship State Schools (Out of State)

The sticker price at a flagship state school that is not in your state is usually higher than at any state school in your state. Its net price may also be higher. While an out-of-state flagship school may offer grants and scholarships to lower the sticker price, these awards are typically modest in comparison to those offered by schools in other college categories. Remember that flagship schools are viewed by the public as attractive options, so these schools attract a large pool of applicants. The more selective a college is, the fewer scholarships it typically offers.

4. Non-Flagship State Schools (Out of State)

Non-flagship schools that are out of state can be a financial fit for many families. Although the sticker price of these schools is higher than the sticker price of state schools within your state, the net price may be equal or lower. Sometimes this is because the school is trying to attract students from out of state. And increasingly, schools in this category are enhancing their merit scholarship offerings.

5. Highly Selective Private Schools

Highly selective private schools are the most prestigious colleges and universities in this country. When most people think of highly selective private schools, they think of schools in the Ivy League, such as Harvard, Princeton, Yale, and Dartmouth. Admission into these schools is extremely competitive. Students must have excellent grades and test scores to be considered for admission.

Most of these schools don't offer merit scholarships based on a student's gifts, strengths, and talents. However, some highly selective private schools offer substantial assistance to families with financial need. They have huge endowments and use that money to help needy families.

Consider the "Harvard Plan." Harvard University has a sticker price of more than $55,000 per year, but the school decided to be a trailblazer for families with financial need. If a family's income is $60,000 or less, a student admitted to Harvard pays nothing. Harvard discounts the entire cost. If the family's income is between $60,000 and $180,000, the most the family pays the school is 10 percent of its income.

While not all highly selective private schools follow the Harvard Plan, many have created their own plans to assist families with financial need. Some schools in this category try to meet 100 percent of a family's assessed need, and some meet this need without requiring a student to obtain student loans. This practice is unheard of among colleges in other categories.

If your child is academically gifted enough to compete for admissions at a highly selective private college, don't eliminate these schools based on their sticker price. Determine the estimated net price at several schools in this category before making a decision.

HIGHLY SELECTIVE SCHOOLS, LOW NET PRICES

Rebecca DuPont was an extremely bright high school student. Her SAT scores were in the top half of the top 1 percent of the country. She had straight As and had taken many honors and advanced placement (AP) classes. Rebecca could also play the violin masterfully and was a student leader in high school. Her teachers, counselors, and peers encouraged her to apply to the most highly selective private schools in the country.

However, Rebecca's mother, Dolores, was not convinced that this was the best option for her daughter. Dolores was a single parent and wanted her daughter to pursue colleges most likely to give her a great deal of scholarship money. She had heard that many of the highly selective private colleges in the country did not offer scholarship money, which is true. With her modest wages and limited savings, she could not come close to paying the very high sticker price of these schools.

However, once Dolores and Rebecca followed the Financial Fit program, they were astounded. Dolores investigated the estimated net price at three highly selective private colleges: Harvard, Brown, and Vanderbilt. Despite the fact that the sticker price at each of these schools was over $55,000, each school's net price was less than $1,000. From then on, Dolores and Rebecca aggressively pursued the highly selective schools.

6. Midsize Private Schools

This is the most unusual category because it contains the fewest schools. Most private colleges are either in the highly selective private schools category or in the next category after this, traditional private schools. Midsize private schools typically have an enrollment of more than 5,000 students. Their sticker prices are lower than colleges in the highly selective private schools category but higher than those in the traditional private schools category. Examples of midsize private schools include Marquette University, Saint Louis University, Bradley University, University of Tampa, and University of Denver.

The schools in the midsize private schools category appear to be costly, but some excellent schools fall into this category, so don't eliminate them from consideration. These colleges also offer attractive merit scholarships and need-based grants. They should be considered like the other categories and only be eliminated if the net prices are beyond your affordability.

7. Traditional Private Schools

This is the largest category of schools. Most colleges and universities in the United States are not state schools or highly selective private schools and fall into this category. Many of these colleges and universities were opened by religious groups in the late 1800s or early 1900s. While some have maintained their original religious identity, others have not. These schools have enrollments ranging from 5,000 students to fewer than 1,000 students.

Traditional private schools in this category are known to offer substantial merit awards. These schools market heavily to attract students. Families are often surprised to learn that the net price of colleges in this category can be affordable.

8. Community College and/or Commuting Options

You can view this category as an option if you don't find financial fits in any of the other seven categories. Community college and commuting options can be so beneficial that we discuss them in detail in Chapter 7.

Organizing by Category

Organizing every college into one of these eight categories is a key aspect of Financial Fit. You can search for colleges within these categories using the Financial Fit College Search tool in the Financial Fit program (www.collegecountdown.com) or in the Appendix at the back of this book.

Once you understand the categories and the variety they represent, you are ready to start working with net price calculators to determine which categories offer the best fit for you.

CHAPTER 6

NET PRICE CALCULATORS AND COMPARING COLLEGE CATEGORIES

N ow that you have determined your affordability threshold and communicated this to your child, and you also have reviewed the Financial Fit college categories, the next step is to start working with net price calculators.

These calculators are a key tool in determining which types of schools represent the best financial fit for your family. Remember that although colleges list costs on their websites, these costs are the sticker prices—and the sticker price is not what families pay for college. The price that you must pay for a college is its net price. The net price is determined after grants, scholarships, federal Direct Loans, and campus employment are deducted from the sticker price.

A net price calculator estimates your net price for a particular college. While an estimated net price is not official, it is a valid estimate and can give you an idea of whether or not a college is affordable.

Because of an initiative established by the U.S. Department of Education, every college in the country must have a net price calculator on its website. This allows families to calculate an estimated net price at any college in the United States at any time.

While this is convenient, it can be confusing because colleges don't use the same universal net price calculator. Some net price calculators estimate price based on specific information, but others do not.

Net price calculators that request the most specific information are usually the most accurate and reliable. An accurate and more reliable net price calculator will take into account both your financial background and your child's academic background. The calculator uses your financial background to determine opportunities for need-based assistance. It uses your child's academic background—usually his or her standardized test scores (SAT or ACT) and grade point average (GPA)—to determine opportunities for scholarships.

A net price calculator might ask you for some or all of this information:

- Whether your child plans to attend college full- or part-time
- Whether your child will commute to college or live on campus
- The number of people in your family
- The number of children in college
- Your household income
- The student's and parents' assets
- Whether your child has served in the military
- Whether your child is twenty-four years of age or older
- Your child's high school GPA
- Your child's class rank
- Your child's SAT critical reading and math scores
- Your child's composite ACT score

The more questions the calculator asks, the higher-quality result you are likely to get.

Although you can use the net price calculator of any college you choose in each of the Financial Fit college categories, you can also consult the list that follows of high-quality net price calculators. These net price calculators will help you determine what a quality net price calculator is like and the type of questions it might ask. (You'll note that these are listed in alphabetical order by their states.)

FRANK'S FAVORITES: QUALITY NET PRICE CALCULATORS

Flagship State Schools

University of Florida
https://npc.collegeboard.org/student/app/ufl

Indiana University-Bloomington
https://npc.collegeboard.org/student/app/indiana

University of Maine
http://umaine.edu/netpricecalculator/

University of North Carolina at Chapel Hill
https://npc.collegeboard.org/student/app/unc

University of Wyoming
https://npc.collegeboard.org/student/app/uwyo

Non-Flagship State Schools

Western Illinois University
http://www.wiu.edu/student_services/financial_aid/netPriceCalculator.php

Ball State University (IN)
https://bsu.studentaidcalculator.com/survey.aspx

Northern Kentucky University
https://nku.studentaidcalculator.com/survey.aspx

Truman State University (MO)
http://netprice.truman.edu/

Marshall University (WV)
https://marshall.studentaidcalculator.com/survey.aspx

Highly Selective Private Schools

Emory University (GA)
https://npc.collegeboard.org/student/app/emory

Amherst College (MA)
https://npc.collegeboard.org/student/app/amherst

Harvard University (MA)
http://isites.harvard.edu/icb/icb.do?keyword=k51861&pageid=icb.page244010

Vassar College (NY)
https://npc.collegeboard.org/student/app/vassar

Vanderbilt University (TN)
https://npc.collegeboard.org/student/app/vanderbilt

Midsize Private Schools

Santa Clara University (CA)
https://scu.studentaidcalculator.com/survey.aspx

University of Tampa (FL)
https://ut.studentaidcalculator.com/survey.aspx

Lewis University (IL)
http://tcc.noellevitz.com/%28S%28erljua5nb3ipqw2li0ih4ibu%29%29/Lewis%20University/Freshman%20Students

Saint Louis University (MO)
https://slu.studentaidcalculator.com/survey.aspx

Marquette University (WI)
https://marquette.studentaidcalculator.com/survey.aspx

Traditional Private Schools

Regis University (CO)
> http://www.regis.edu/rc.asp?page=financial
> .calculator

North Central College (IL)
> https://northcentralcollege.studentaidcalcula
> tor.com/survey.aspx

St. Ambrose College (IA)
> http://www.sau.edu/Financial_Aid_Office/
> Resources/Net_Price_Calculator/Freshmen_
> Student_Calculator.html

Saint Mary's University of Minnesota
> http://www.smumn.edu/undergraduate-home/
> tuition-financial-aid/net-price-calculator/npc

St. Bonaventure (NY)
> http://tcc.noellevitz.com/(S(lkciuiud25yg
> 240wrauhze13))/St-Bonaventure-University/
> FreshmanStudents

Comparing College Categories

To get an idea of which college categories are affordable for your family, you should test out a few net price calculators in every category. It helps to have a list of all colleges in the country divided into the Financial Fit college categories. You can search for colleges within these categories using the Financial Fit College Search tool in the Financial Fit program (www.collegecountdown.com). They are also printed in the Appendix of this book. This helps you rule out categories that are not affordable. We call the Financial Fit college categories that you can afford "categorical fits."

To record your findings, you can create a category comparison table or complete one online using the Financial Fit software program. A blank version of such a chart is on page 80. Complete the net price calculator at a few schools for each category, then enter the estimate in the right-hand column. (Note that you do not calculate commuting/community college in the category comparison table; that category is reviewed if none of the first seven are affordable.)

Table 6.1: Category Comparison Table	
School Name	**Net Price Estimate**
Flagship State Schools (In State)	
Non-Flagship State Schools (In State)	
Flagship State Schools (Out of State)	
Non-Flagship State Schools (Out of State)	

Table 6.1: Category Comparison Table, cont.

School Name	Net Price Estimate
Highly Selective Private Schools	
Midsize Private Schools	
Traditional Private Schools	

Compare the net prices of the colleges you select in each of the categories. The net prices for schools within a category should be similar. Thus, you should be able to determine categories of schools that do not appear to be affordable, those with net prices consistently above your affordability threshold. Remember, don't eliminate a category before you choose two or three colleges and use each of those schools' net price calculators.

IS A COLLEGE THE RIGHT "FIT"?

Right College, Right Price suggests that the right college "fits" your child in all ways. The right college should be a financial fit, but it should also be an academic fit and a "feel fit," which means that the atmosphere of the college feels right to your child.

In considering whether a college is an academic fit, check whether it has the academic programs that your child wants to pursue. Is the academic profile of the student body in line with your child's academic profile? Compare your child's GPA in high school to the median GPA of the college population. Also compare your child's ACT/SAT scores with the median scores of students at the college. If your child's GPA and test scores match up with the median population, then the school is probably an academic fit.

Determining whether a college has the right "feel fit" is not as easy. If a college has the right feel fit, students can imagine themselves as part of the college culture. Consider whether a college has programs beyond those in the classroom that will engage your son or daughter. Does the general personality of the student body seem compatible with your child's personality? You can usually determine feel fit when you visit colleges and talk to students, professors, and admissions counselors.

Academic fit and feel fit should not be considered until you have found colleges that are financial fits. What good is a college that fits your child perfectly academically if it jeopardizes his or her financial future? We'll discuss academic fit and feel

....

    fit in more detail in Chapter 8, "Narrow Down Your
    List of Colleges."

....

Financial Fit in Action

The results of your category comparison will reflect your personal situation. The following five examples of families who followed the Financial Fit college search program show the variety of results you may get.

The Sebastians

The Sebastians live in Illinois and have two children: Josh, a high school junior, and Melissa, a seventh-grade student. The parents have a combined income of $90,000. They have saved $20,000 for emergencies and have a $10,000 529 prepay tuition plan for each child. Josh is a good student. His GPA is 3.6 and his best ACT score is 26. The Sebastians completed Worksheet 1 and determined that their affordability threshold, the maximum amount they can pay per year for college, is $14,000.

The table below shows the estimated net prices for colleges in each category using the net price calculator on each college's website. To make certain the comparison was accurate, the family included the estimated net price without student loan and work options. They then subtracted the $5,500 Direct Loan that all freshmen are eligible for and a $1,500 job on campus. They assumed that Josh would be able to find a job and earn this much money per year, which he could use to pay miscellaneous expenses. Thus, the net price estimates reflect the following at each college:

Sticker Price – Grants, Scholarships, On-Campus Job, and
Maximum Amount Allowed in Direct Loans = Net Price

Table 6.2: Net Prices per Category for the Sebastian Family	
School Name	**Net Price Estimate**
Flagship State Schools (In State)	
University of Illinois at Urbana	$26,028
N/A	
N/A	
Non-Flagship State Schools (In State)	
Southern Illinois at Carbondale	$12,286
Illinois State	$12,586
Northern Illinois	$12,900
Flagship State Schools (Out of State)	
Purdue University	$34,126
Michigan State University	$35,170
University of Wisconsin–Madison	$31,491
Non-Flagship State Schools (Out of State)	
Grand Valley State University	$10,668
Truman State University	$8,941
University of Northern Iowa	$11,287

School Name	Net Price Estimate
Table 6.2: Net Prices per Category for the Sebastian Family, cont.	
Highly Selective Private Schools	
Stanford University	$2,900
Vanderbilt University	$3,592
N/A	
Midsize Private Schools	
Marquette University	$28,162
University of Denver	$23,550
Saint Louis University	$25,846
Traditional Private Schools	
Saint Mary's in Minnesota	$15,500
Hanover College	$12,719
Saint Xavier University	$12,557

The Results

The estimated net price at the flagship state school, the University of Illinois at Urbana, is $26,028. Since Illinois has only one flagship school, the Sebastians could not test other schools in this category. University of Illinois was not a financial fit. The estimated net prices at flagship state schools that were out of state were also too high. The Sebastians eliminated these two categories.

The Sebastians were encouraged by the estimated net prices of non-flagship state schools. As they saw on their chart, non-flagships both in and out of state had net prices lower than their family's affordability threshold. The Sebastians were eager to explore a number of schools in this category.

In addition, the Sebastians examined the net prices of colleges in the highly selective private schools category and were amazed at the results. They realized, however, that schools in this category would not be an academic fit for Josh. He most likely would not be admitted to these schools, so the Sebastians eliminated this category.

They also eliminated the midsize private schools category because the estimated net price of these schools was beyond what they could afford. However, the Sebastians found potential financial fits in the traditional private school category.

Based on the results of category comparison, the family planned to pursue colleges in these categories:

- Non-flagship schools (in state)
- Non-flagship schools (out of state)
- Traditional private colleges

The Sebastians were ready to move on to the next step. From the end of Josh's junior year and throughout the summer before his senior year, they would peruse college websites, exchange email with college admissions counselors, and visit college campuses. Now that they had discovered college categories that were a financial fit for their family, they could look for colleges within these categories that were an academic fit and at which Josh felt comfortable.

The Duchaines

The Duchaines are residents of Ohio. While their family income of $110,000 is fairly high, they have four children, and two of their children, Joseph and Sharon, are twins headed to college at the same time. Their two other children are both in high school, one a sophomore and the other a freshman. Joseph and Sharon are both B students with ACT scores of 22 and 23.

After completing Worksheet 1, the Duchaines realized that they could afford only $8,000 per year per child, even though they had been regularly saving for college and had accumulated $35,000. They were very concerned about being able to afford to send all four children to college and were committed to conserving some of those savings for their younger children.

Table 6.3: Net Prices per Category for the Duchaine Family	
School Name	**Net Price Estimate**
Flagship State Schools (In State)	
Ohio State University	$19,847
N/A	
N/A	
Non-Flagship State Schools (In State)	
Bowling Green State University	$13,900
University of Akron	$10,369
University of Cincinnati	$16,400
Flagship State Schools (Out of State)	
Michigan State University	$35,170
University of Illinois at Urbana	$33,489
Arizona State University	$31,147

Table 6.3: Net Prices per Category for the Duchaine Family, cont.	
School Name	**Net Price Estimate**
Non-Flagship State Schools (Out of State)	
University of Illinois at Chicago	$26,271
Ball State University	$28,130
Michigan Tech University	$18,229
Highly Selective Private Schools	
N/A	
N/A	
N/A	
Midsize Private Schools	
DePaul University	$23,218
Drake University	$22,990
Creighton University	$18,107
Traditional Private Schools	
St. Bonaventure University	$20,275
Saint Ambrose University	$18,255
Ohio Dominican University	$13,850

The Results

After they completed the college comparison table for schools in each category, the Duchaines realized that none of the estimated net prices from these schools was affordable. (They did not view schools in the highly selective private school category because neither of their children would be accepted at these schools.)

As you recall, according to Financial Fit, you have two fallback options in such a case: the commuting option and the community college option. The Duchaines moved on to these options. Joseph did not want to attend a community college and instead chose the commuting option.

The Duchaines live in Cleveland, and Joseph was able to find a few local four-year schools where he could live at home. Joseph planned to pursue a degree in elementary education, and these schools met his academic needs as well. John Carroll University in Cleveland had an estimated net price of $6,470 if Joseph commuted to school and obtained Direct Loans. It was obviously a financial fit.

Sharon had not yet decided on a major and was very comfortable attending a local community college. The family's net price for Sharon was zero because she was able to borrow enough in Direct Loans to pay her tuition.

The Ramonos

The Ramonos have three children: Nancy, a junior in high school, Victoria, a sophomore in high school, and Brian, a freshman in high school. Their family income is $60,000, and they have saved $5,000 for college. Nancy is an outstanding student with a 4.0 GPA and an ACT score of 34.

The Ramonos know they will be able to do very little to help their children pay for college. After completing Worksheet 1, they determined that they could spend $4,000 per year per child on college.

The Ramonos realized that Nancy was academically gifted, so they wanted her to apply to schools in the highly selective private school category. Since these schools have the highest sticker prices—$55,000 or more in many cases—families with limited means often don't consider them as options. However, because these schools have extraordinary endowments, they can support students from families with limited financial means.

The Ramonos had read about the Harvard Plan and were encouraged. They learned that if their family income is $60,000 or less and their child is admitted to Harvard, their net price would be zero. If their income is between $60,000 and $180,000, their net price at Harvard would usually be 10 percent of their income. While not all highly selective private schools have programs like Harvard's, many of them use their significant resources to help families with financial need.

The Ramonos decided to focus only on the highly selective private school category. When they included the $5,500 Direct Loan option and a $1,500 per year job for Nancy, the estimated net prices of three schools in this category were as follows:

Table 6.4: Net Prices for Highly Selective Private Schools for the Ramonos Family	
School Name	**Net Price Estimate**
Highly Selective Private Schools	
Duke University	$1,600
Harvard University	$0
Yale University	$0

It is important to note that no matter how academically gifted a student is, admission to schools in this category is extremely competitive. Nancy applied to seven schools in this category and also had a fallback plan. A local traditional private college offered Nancy a full scholarship based on her grades and test scores. She could commute to school and have a zero net price.

Nancy was accepted at four of the highly selective private colleges. She chose Yale and had a zero net price. Amazing!

The Morettis

Together, the Morettis earned $130,000 and had saved $27,000 for college. They did not have to worry about paying tuition, however. Mrs. Moretti's mother planned to pay for college for each of her three grandchildren.

The Morettis followed the Financial Fit program even though they knew that they were going to send their son David to the college of his choice. They wanted him to appreciate the importance of making good financial decisions and compare the net prices at several schools. They told him that their affordability threshold was $25,000 per year.

David was a good student. He had a 3.9 GPA and an SAT Critical Reading and Math score of 1550. While David would not likely be accepted at schools in the highly selective private school category, he would be accepted at most schools in the other categories. Since David did not want to attend a small college, his parents investigated schools in the two categories that most interested him: flagship state schools both in and out of Colorado, their home state. They also investigated schools in the midsize private school category.

Table 6.5: Net Prices per Category for the Moretti Family	
School Name	**Net Price Estimate**
Flagship State Schools (In State)	
University of Colorado Boulder	$17,747
N/A	
N/A	

Table 6.5: Net Prices per Category for the Moretti Family, cont.	
School Name	**Net Price Estimate**
Flagship State Schools (Out of State)	
University of Kansas	$23,686
University of Nebraska	$22,312
University of Washington	$34,543
Midsize Private Schools	
Creighton University	$23,525
University of Denver	$26,050
Loyola University Chicago	$28,750

The Results

Using the results shown in the category comparison table, David decided to apply to Creighton University, the University of Denver, the University of Kansas, and the University of Nebraska. These schools all matched David's preferences in terms of his major, which was business. After visiting each school, he decided to attend Creighton because he felt most comfortable there. Even though his final college decision was not bound by affordability, his parents valued the exercise and wanted David to see how important it is to make prudent financial decisions.

Angela Johnson

Angela grew up in a single-parent household, and her mother had many personal problems. Angela had little parental support of any kind and no financial resources to pay for college. However, Angela was a better-than-average student and was active in clubs and organizations.

She was also a high school cheerleader. During her senior year, Angela was captain of the squad.

Angela created a resume to maximize her benefits. (We'll discuss resumes and other techniques your child can use to showcase their strengths in Chapter 13.) She also met with several college admissions counselors when they visited her high school during the fall of her senior year. The counselors were captivated with Angela's ability to overcome so many personal obstacles. They were also impressed with her strong academic performance and commitment to the cheerleading squad.

Angela followed the Financial Fit program. She discovered that, except for community colleges, she would need significant financial support to attend a college in any category. Angela qualified for the federal Pell Grant and a state grant. (We'll discuss financial aid in Chapter 9.) She was willing to obtain the maximum amount allowed in Direct Loans ($5,500) and to find a job on campus to cover personal expenses. However, these resources did not cover the entire estimated net price of college.

Angela could have attended a community college, but she really wanted to leave home. Her high school guidance counselor and the college admissions counselors at St. Ambrose College in Iowa (a traditional private college) and Truman State University in Missouri (an out-of-state non-flagship school) helped her reach her goal. Impressed with Angela, these counselors personally worked with financial aid officers to create award packages that allowed Angela to attend college with no out-of-pocket cost.

This kind of outcome does not happen on its own, however. Angela had a compelling story and worked hard to develop positive relationships with adults who were all working on her behalf.

Making It Work

Each of these examples illustrates the importance of using Financial Fit to find a group of affordable college options. These families were able to save time, energy, and money by focusing from the start on those categories of schools that appeared to be affordable.

Before they applied to schools, these families did the following:

1. Assessed their affordability
2. Communicated their affordability to their child
3. Determined the estimated price of each Financial Fit college category
4. Eliminated unaffordable categories
5. Kept the affordable categories

By doing so, they were able to determine which category (or categories) was the best fit.

The best fit isn't always one of the first seven, though, as the Duchaines showed. In the next chapter, we'll take a closer look at the eighth category—when attending a commuting or community college is the best choice for your student.

KEY POINTS

- While all colleges have a net price calculator on their website, these calculators are not all the same. Some are more accurate and reliable than others. Net price calculators that ask for detailed academic and financial information are usually the most accurate.
- To learn which college categories are affordable, "test" a few colleges in each category by determining your estimated net price.
- Compare the net prices of colleges in each category using a category comparison table.

CHAPTER 7

CONSIDER THE COMMUTING AND COMMUNITY COLLEGE OPTIONS

I f the net price of college in the first seven categories is out of reach for your family, what do you do then? When you follow the Financial Fit program, the next step is considering the commuting and community college options.

Commuting

Terry's family has determined that they could afford to pay $10,000 per year for college. Terry wants to attend Viterbo University, a local traditional private school with a sticker price of $34,000 per year, $8,000 of which is the cost of room and board. Terry's family is not eligible for need-based awards, but Terry has received a merit award from this college of $10,000 per year. Terry believes he can get an on–campus job and earn $2,000 per year. The following is the net price of Viterbo University for Terry and his family:

$34,000 tuition and fees, and room and board –
$10,000 merit award – $5,500 Direct Loan – $2,000 job =
$16,500 net price

The net price of this college is $6,500 more per year than Terry's family can afford. However, if Terry does not live on campus, the net price of this school is $8,500, which is under his family's affordability threshold. If he can be convinced to commute, Terry gets to attend his dream school and the cost does not put him and his family in financial jeopardy.

Using the commuting option, you can significantly reduce the net price of college if your child lives at home and commutes to school each day. Room and board is expensive, between $8,000 and $10,000 at most schools. (See Figure 7.1.)

Commuting is more common than you might believe. About 86 percent of college and university students commute to school. While some of these students live in off-campus apartments, many of them live at home.

Convincing your son or daughter to become a commuter might not be easy. Many students have their hearts set on living on campus. These same students may become determined to attend a particular school. This type of thinking has caused the student debt crisis. In choosing a college, affordability is paramount, and commuting is one way to significantly reduce costs.

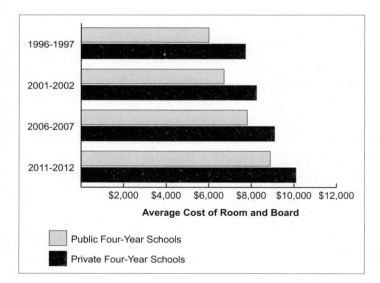

Figure 7.1: Increase in the Average Cost of Room and Board at Public and Private Four-Year Schools

How to Convince Your Child That Commuting Is a Good Option

Some students would rather live at home than on a college campus. They enjoy the comforts and quiet of home and do not want to be part of a bustling campus twenty-four hours a day, seven days a week. These students may also have a part-time job that they want to keep while in college or close friends who are commuting to local schools. If your child would rather live at home, convincing him or her of the benefits of commuting will be easy.

However, this might not be the case with your child. Many students are not in favor of commuting at first. They would rather live on a college campus and experience all that college has to offer. You may have to convince your child that commuting is a practical and responsible option. One of the best ways to do this is to point out the impact their debt will have on their life after college. Students aren't always the best at seeing the big picture related to debt, but showing them the numbers in a realistic way can have an eye-opening effect.

Suppose your child is Terry in the example you just read, and he is adamant about living on campus while attending college. You could say, "Terry, these are your options. We can afford to provide you with $10,000 per year for college. You can attend Viterbo, live at home, and have a debt of $27,000 when you graduate. Or, you can live on campus and have a debt closer to $60,000 upon graduation.

"If you borrow the $27,000 using Direct Loans, your monthly payment for ten years will be less than $300 per month. If you obtain a private loan for the extra $30,000 you need to live on campus, your monthly payment will be $700 or more per month. So what would you rather do? Live at home with us for ten years after college while you're paying back your student loans, or live with us while in college and then get your own apartment when you graduate?" For Terry, most likely the answer will be easy.

Commuting to a Private School

When many families determine that they need to lower the cost of college, they gravitate toward state-supported schools in their own state, which have a lower sticker price than private colleges. This is certainly an option, but it may not always be the best one for your son or daughter.

If your child functions better in a smaller environment where the learning community is more nurturing, he or she may be most comfortable in a private school. To make these schools affordable, consider having your child commute to school. In many cases, students who attend private schools and commute are still eligible for need-based and merit-based money, which may make attending a private school and commuting more affordable than attending a state-supported institution and living on campus.

If during the college search process, you find that many schools on your category comparison table are unaffordable, add a column to the chart for the commuting option. Have your son or daughter identify a few schools that are close enough to commute to. Determine the estimated price for these schools without room and board, and include it on the chart. If you can't find a fit in any of the other categories of schools—schools where your child would live on campus—the commuting option could be a great option, one that might be your financial fit.

The bottom line is that you and your child must build a sound plan for college together. Doing this will enable your son or daughter to attend an excellent four-year school without accumulating unnecessary and damaging debt.

COMMUTING MAY BE THE BEST OPTION

While I was waiting for the tires on my car to be replaced the other day, I saw a young man whom I often see with his family at church. I introduced myself and learned that his name was Stephen. He was a recent college graduate who had just begun a new job.

With the economy as challenging as it is, I'm always pleased to learn of a recent college graduate finding employment. I asked Stephen about his undergraduate experience and which college he had graduated from. Stephen graduated from a local school. He lived at home and commuted to school.

"What do you think of that decision?" I asked.

Stephen's response was quite telling. He said, "I think everyone my age wants to live away from home at a big university on an attractive college campus, but honestly, I know I made the right decision. I have so many friends who went away to college and had a great time. Now they all wish they were me because they're suffocating with huge student loans—and I don't have any!

"The college I chose gave me lots of scholarship money, and because I come from a single-parent home, I received some state aid. I used the money I had saved from the job I had in high school to help pay my tuition and I worked every summer. I don't have any debt."

Stephen's story is a prime example of how, for many families, the commuting option is a viable way to find affordable college options and pay for college without accumulating excessive debt.

The Community College Option

Like the commuting option, the community college option may be right for your child, especially if your family does not receive enough need-based grants or merit awards, or both, from the colleges in the other categories. Whenever the net price of other colleges is out of reach, a community college can be an excellent choice for the first two years.

Four out of ten college students—more than six million—begin their college education at a community college. They do this for a variety of reasons, not the least of which is cost. Tuition and fees at a community college are much lower than at public and private colleges and universities. (See Figure 7.2.)

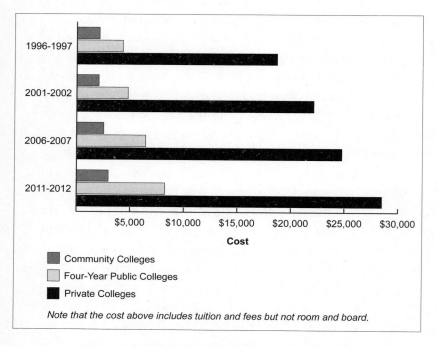

Figure 7.2: Cost of Community College versus Public and Private Schools

Some students choose community colleges because of the wide array of programs these schools offer, including very specific career-based training. These programs, often called vocational programs, prepare students to enter the workforce in two years or less. Students enrolled in vocational programs receive a certificate or an associate's degree upon graduation. They are then ready to enter the workforce and begin earning a living.

Many other students attend a community college and then transfer to a four-year school after graduation. These students often take core courses, courses that are required by students of all majors, at the community college and then take the courses required by their major at a four-year college.

Most community colleges have an open admission policy, meaning that they accept all students who have graduated from high school, regardless of their GPA or test scores. A community college is a great place for students who need to improve their GPAs. When students obtain an associate's degree and transfer to a four-year school, the school looks only at the grades they earned while at the community college. On top of that, the more than one thousand community colleges in the United States are mostly in the center of towns and cities, so public transportation is readily available.

While attending a community college offers many benefits, we'll focus in this section on how a community college can lower the comprehensive net price of the four years it takes to earn a bachelor's degree and make a four-year college a financial fit in the last two years.

Financial Benefits of Attending a Community College

The community college option might be the best for you and your child if you can't find financial fits within the other college categories—flagship in-state schools, flagship out-of-state schools, non-flagship in-state schools, non-flagship state schools, highly selective private schools, midsize private schools, and traditional private schools.

While your child is at the community college, you can take what you would have spent for the first two years at the four-year school and place that amount in savings for the final two years. This is a tremendous benefit! Imagine how you could better manage the overall costs for your child if you could minimize or eliminate your out-of-pocket costs for two years. This is what the community college option allows you to do.

Without knowing anything about you financially, we can predict the net price of a local community college for your child—zero. Remember that all students who file a FAFSA are eligible for up to $5,500 in a Direct Loan for their freshman year and $6,500 for their sophomore year. These loan amounts are more than enough to cover the tuition and fees at most community colleges as long as you don't choose one that is out of your district. If the community college is in your district and your child qualifies for the federal Pell Grant or perhaps a state grant, he or she might not need to obtain any loans.

Merit Awards for Transfer Students

Many schools now offer merit awards to students transferring from community colleges. These awards are not based on a student's test scores and high school GPA, but on a student's performance while attending the community college. This means that if your son or daughter attends a community college and receives excellent grades, he or she may be eligible for a merit scholarship for the third and fourth years of college.

Don Sommers and his parents, David and Rita, realized that paying for college was going to be challenging. The family has six children, and Don is the oldest. David and Rita explained to their children that they would not be able to offer them much financial assistance for college.

After following the Financial Fit program, Don and his parents decided that his best option was community college. Don worked during the summer and used his own savings along with a modest student loan of $1,000 each year to pay his tuition.

When he graduated, he transferred to a local private college so he could live at home and commute to college each day. (As we discussed in the last section, a student can eliminate the cost of room and board, which is usually between $8,000 and $10,000 per year, by living at home.) The private four-year college has a sticker price of $25,000, which included tuition and fees but not room and board.

Don earned exceptional grades while he attended the community college, so the private college offered him a merit scholarship of $6,000. This brought down his net price to $19,000. Because of his parents' limited financial means, Don received a state grant of $4,500. Now his net price was $14,500. Don obtained the maximum Direct Loan of $7,500 for the junior year. This brought down his net price to $7,000.

The Sommers learned from the affordability questionnaire that they were eligible for a $2,500 tax credit. They determined that in addition to this credit, they could contribute $1,500 for Don's college. Their affordability threshold was therefore $4,000.

Now the remaining money needed was $3,000, which Don did not have. He contacted the four-year college and explained his situation. The college added a $3,000 need-based grant, which allowed him to attend there without placing himself or his parents in financial jeopardy.

Let's review Don and his family's four-year college financial plan:

- Years 1 and 2: Don attends community college and pays for it with the money he saved from work and a $1,000 Direct Loan each year.
- Years 3 and 4: Don uses his parents' $4,000 per year contribution and the other resources we discussed. He borrows $7,500 in Direct Loans for his junior year and $7,500 in Direct Loans for his senior year.

Over the four years, Don accumulates debt of only $17,000. His parents have not borrowed any money, which will help them prepare for the college expenses of their other five children.

The Bottom Line

While commuting or community college may not be your first choice, either can be a great choice if the first seven categories don't meet your financial threshold. Families should always consider the community college and commuting options before they make their final college choice, because they can achieve great results with these options while avoiding the looming debt they'd face by choosing a college out of their affordability.

KEY POINTS

- Having your child commute is a great way to reduce the net price of college.
- Some students would rather live on campus than at home, so convincing your child to commute may not be easy. Point out how much the cost of college is reduced without fees for room and board; explain why commuting is a better option than accumulating excessive debt.
- If you think your child would thrive in a smaller, nurturing environment, consider having him or her commute to a local private school.
- Attending a commuting college for the first two years is a great option if the price of four-year schools is out of reach for your family.
- Many students take core courses at a community college and then transfer to a four-year school where they take courses related to their major.
- Because all students can take unsubsidized Direct Loans, the net price of community college is zero.
- Many four-year schools now offer merit awards to students who transfer from a community college.

CHAPTER 8

NARROW DOWN YOUR LIST OF COLLEGES

Before you move on to the next step in Financial Fit and narrow down your list of potential schools, let's review the steps you've completed so far:

- You assessed how much money you can afford to spend on college.
- You communicated this affordability to your child so you are all on the same page.
- You analyzed college categories and determined the estimated net price of several colleges in each category.
- Using a category comparison table, you compared the estimated net price of colleges in each category to see which categories appear to fit you financially and which are out of reach.
- You determined if you need the community college or the commuting option, or both, as part of your application strategy.

By now, you have probably identified colleges that are a financial fit for your family. Before you did this, your child had more than 2,000 four-year college options in the United States. However, after you eliminated college categories that are unaffordable, your list became more manageable. Now you need to narrow down this list even more so you can avoid applying to too many schools, which can be expensive and time-consuming.

To show you a great way to work through how to narrow down your options, we'll follow Theresa on her journey. While you might not make the same choices she did, note how Theresa approached narrowing down her list because it is a great way to move from many options to the right colleges for you.

Case Study: Theresa Roland

When Theresa Roland was a junior in high school, her parents, Larry and Deb Roland, helped her determine that these five Financial Fit college categories appeared to be affordable options:

- Community college and/or commuting options
- Traditional private schools
- Highly selective private schools
- Non–flagship state schools (in state)
- Non–flagship state schools (out of state)

Consider Academic Fit

The Rolands' next step was to eliminate categories of schools that were not an academic fit for their daughter. Schools that are an academic fit for your child have his or her desired major or program of study. They also have an academic profile that is similar to your child's. A school often lists its academic profile as a range of its students' high school GPAs, ACT composite scores, and SAT scores. Keep in mind that your child has a better chance of being awarded a merit scholarship from a school where he or she is in the top 25 percent of the academic profile.

The Rolands were surprised to discover that the prestigious colleges in the highly selective private schools category were a financial fit for their family. However, they were aware that only a small number of students who apply to these schools are admitted. Theresa did not fit the academic profile required for admission to these schools. She had a combined SAT score of 1200, an ACT composite score of 24, and a GPA of 3.25. Students admitted to schools in this category have test scores and grades that are much higher than this. Therefore, the Rolands eliminated the highly selective private school category.

Consider Location

Theresa and her family considered location next. Theresa decided that if she lived on campus, she wanted to be close enough to visit home on weekends and holidays. Because of this, the Rolands decided to investigate schools that were relatively close to home—in their home state of Indiana and three surrounding states: Illinois, Ohio, and Michigan.

Theresa searched for colleges using the Financial Fit College Search tool in the Financial Fit program (www.collegecountdown.com) and chose two non-flagship state schools in Indiana and two non-flagship schools in each of the three other states. As a fallback plan in case the official net price of schools in the other categories turned out to be unaffordable, the Rolands decided that Theresa should also apply to two schools from the community college or commuter category.

Community colleges were an excellent financial fit for the family, but Theresa wanted to attend the same school for four years. She decided to pursue the commuting option instead and investigated schools that were fairly close to her home. Theresa chose two local schools in this category that offered a major in biology.

So far, Theresa considered applying to ten schools: two commuting options, two non-flagship state schools, and six schools in the non-flagship out of state category. Next she had to choose schools in the traditional private schools category.

This is the largest of all the Financial Fit college categories, so selecting schools from this category is not easy. To make the choice even more difficult, the schools within this category are similar. Most have a low student-teacher ratio, a relatively small campus, and a nurturing atmosphere. Theresa and her family once again focused on schools in their home state and in the three surrounding states, but there were still many schools to choose from. Theresa made a list of schools in this category—but it was a very long list.

Ask for Recommendations

Theresa needed help, so she made an appointment with her high school guidance counselor. Her school had an upcoming College Night, and representatives from more than 200 colleges and universities would be there. Theresa wanted to speak to a representative from each school on her list, so she needed to narrow down her options.

When Theresa met with her guidance counselor, the counselor was impressed with the process that Theresa had followed so far. Theresa said, "I'm interested in your thoughts about small private colleges from Indiana, Illinois, Ohio, and Michigan. You know that I plan to major in biology." Theresa showed her guidance counselor her list and asked her for recommendations.

The guidance counselor chose eight traditional private schools from Theresa's list, two from each state, based on recommendations from former students. This was a tremendous help. Now Theresa had a plan. She narrowed down the more than 2,000 four-year colleges in the country to eighteen schools in Indiana, Ohio, Michigan, and Illinois.

Speak to College Representatives

Theresa spoke with representatives from these eighteen schools at College Night. She introduced herself as a high school junior who was just beginning the college exploration process. She explained that she was considering their college because it appeared to fit her family financially. Then she asked them all the same question, "Could you tell me something about your biology program?"

She was impressed with some of their responses but not with others. Based on the information they provided about their college's biology program, Theresa was able to narrow down her list of colleges once again. Ten schools remained on her list: two commuter schools, four non-flagship state schools, and four traditional private colleges.

So to this point, Theresa and her family had managed to narrow down her list to ten schools because:

1. They chose categories of schools with an estimated net price that appeared to be affordable.

2. They considered whether the schools in each category were an academic fit.
3. They chose schools in a location that appealed to Theresa.
4. Theresa asked her guidance counselor for recommendations.
5. Theresa asked representatives to give her details about their school's biology program.

Now they needed to take the next steps toward deciding which schools to apply to.

Consult the Fiske Guide to Colleges

The Rolands needed to narrow down Theresa's list even more, so they consulted the *Fiske Guide to Colleges*, a book that gives a detailed description of the country's best and most interesting colleges. Theresa's high school guidance counselor recommended this book as a good resource to learn more about the colleges that remained on her list. Theresa read about the ten colleges on her list, noting things she liked and didn't like about each school. She then eliminated four colleges from her list. She and her parents made plans to visit the remaining six colleges.

Visit College Campuses

The Rolands planned to visit colleges on three days during the spring and summer. They designated the first day to visit the two colleges that Theresa could commute to. On the second day, they planned to visit the non-flagship school in Indiana and a traditional private college not far from that state school. On the third day the family would travel to Michigan to visit a non-flagship state school out of state and a school from the traditional private schools category. They contacted each admissions office in advance to arrange a tour of the biology labs as well as a meeting with a biology professor and, if possible, a student majoring in biology.

During their visits, they planned to see each school's residence halls, fitness center, student center, library, and computer labs. They wanted to learn as much as possible about the school's social and cultural activities. They planned to take notes about what did and did not impress them at each college.

COLLEGE SEARCH TIP

A word of caution: Don't visit schools that are not a financial fit. If you do, your child may fall in love with a particular school and insist on going there even though it is unaffordable. Only visit schools that you have determined are affordable. This way, if your child decides that a particular school is perfect, this school can become his or her top choice.

Ask If Net Price Calculators Are Reliable

They also made a plan for each visit related to affordability. They would ask a college admissions officer at each school a question: "Is the estimated net price from your college's net price calculator an accurate estimate of our official net price?"

The response to this question is very important. The work you do during the Planning Phase of Financial Fit hinges on reliable net price estimates. Your goal is to turn these estimates into reality. If you get the impression from a college admissions counselor that the college's net price calculator might not be reliable, that college may not be a viable option for your child.

Prepare to Apply to Schools

When Theresa returned to school in the fall, she was prepared to apply to four colleges. The Rolands were confident that the net price calculators at these schools were reliable. Theresa planned to apply to one school that she could commute to in case the official net prices of the remaining three schools were higher than the family had estimated.

Of the remaining three schools, Theresa applied to one non-flagship state school in Michigan. Although she was generally more impressed with the smaller schools when she visited the campuses, this particular school organized its residence halls by students' majors, which she thought might benefit her academically. Theresa applied to two traditional private colleges where she had been impressed by the friendliness of the students and professors.

Putting It All Together

Narrowing down a list of potential college from hundreds or thousands to just a few may seem daunting. But by following these simple steps, Teresa (and you) can manage this quite effectively:

- Consider academic fit.
- Consider location.
- Ask for recommendations.
- Speak to college representatives.
- Consult the *Fiske Guide to Colleges* or refer to the online resource, Fiske Interactive Online, at www.collegecountdown.com.
- Visit college campuses.
- Ask if net price calculators are reliable.
- Prepare to apply to schools.

In Part 3, you will learn how to turn your estimated net price into reality and eventually how to make a final college choice—your right college, right price!

KEY POINTS

- Aim to apply to four to six schools. Once you have a list of schools that are a financial fit, narrow down your list by choosing those that are an academic fit.
- Schools that are an academic fit have your child's major and an academic profile similar to your child's.
- Your child should consider the location of the schools remaining on the list and consider how far he or she is willing to travel.
- The *Fiske Guide to Colleges* and its online equivalent, Fiske Interactive Online, are great resources to use to help narrow down your list of colleges.

Part 3

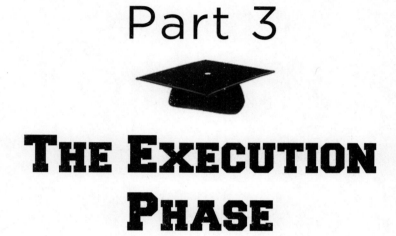

THE EXECUTION PHASE

UNDERSTAND EXPECTED FAMILY CONTRIBUTION (EFC) AND ITS RELATIONSHIP TO FINANCIAL AID

As you move into the Execution Phase, you begin to work with the financial aid system for the first time. This, in fact, is when most families first begin looking at the issue of college cost. So if you have been following the Financial Fit program, you are in a great place to start this phase. Still there are many important and confusing steps in the financial aid part of the process, so we'll walk you through each one with the Financial Fit methodology in mind.

Many students depend on financial aid to attend college. Your family's need for financial aid is determined when you file the FAFSA, which determines your Expected Family Contribution (EFC). In fact, this equation has traditionally been the cornerstone of the financial aid process:

Cost of Attendance − Expected Family Contribution = Need

Unfortunately, today this equation contributes to the confusion many families experience regarding the cost of college and the amount of money they will receive in financial aid. To understand what makes this equation confusing, you need to understand the history of the EFC and the financial-aid delivery system.

Expected Family Contribution (EFC)

The EFC is a number that is calculated when a family completes and files the FAFSA, a document created by the U.S. Department of Education. Historically, when a family learned their EFC number, they viewed it as what they were expected to pay the college. Thus, when the EFC is subtracted from the cost of attendance in the equation above, the result is "need." In the past, "need" was the amount of money a family required in financial aid to attend that college.

This equation was very useful for families up until the late 1980s. Until then, the EFC was exactly that—the amount of money a family had to pay for their child to attend college. The cost of college was not nearly as high back then, and financial aid programs were available to meet 100 percent of a family's need. These programs included federal grants, state grants, college need-based awards, work-study jobs, and subsidized student loans.

Today, these programs still exist, but they no longer fulfill the "need" determined by this equation. Why? The cost of college has risen exponentially while the amount of money awarded by these programs has not. A greater disparity now exists between the amount of money a student receives in financial aid and the amount of money the student needs to attend college. In many cases today, colleges do not have enough money to meet 100 percent of a student's need.

If 100 percent of a family's need is not met, EFC no longer means what it was intended to mean. For example, suppose Max wants to attend a college with a sticker price of $30,000 per year. His family's EFC number is 1,500. Insert these amounts into the equation:

Cost of Attendance − Expected Family Contribution = Need

$$\$30,000 - \$1,500 = \$28,500$$

So Max's need is $28,500. Max receives $18,000 in federal and state grants, a campus job, and student loans. (We'll discuss the types of financial aid later. Educational loans are discussed in Chapter 15.) Max's remaining need is now $10,500. The college he would like to attend is only able to offer him $4,000 per year in a need-based grant, so Max is still short $6,500 per year. Thus, the amount of money that Max's family must pay out of pocket is not his EFC of $1,500 but actually $8,000.

So as you can see, your EFC does not equal your affordability. Your family's EFC number is still useful today, though. This is because colleges use this number to determine whether you are eligible for certain financial aid programs, which we'll discuss in this chapter. Learning your EFC using FAFSA4caster.com before you file the FAFSA can be advantageous. Although the FAFSA cannot be filed until January 1st, estimating your EFC using FAFSA4caster.com will allow you to determine aid programs that you might be eligible for and how they could affect your net price. Some net price calculators even allow you to use your EFC number instead of completing all the required financial questions.

Variables Used to Calculate EFC

Four primary variables are used to calculate an EFC number:

- Parents' income (from the tax return of the year prior to the student's enrollment in college)
- Parents' assets (at the time the FAFSA is completed)
- Student's income (from the tax return of the year prior to the student's enrollment in college)
- Student's assets (at the time the FAFSA is completed)

Parents' Income

You will be asked questions about your income when you file the FAFSA (for your official EFC) and on FAFSA4caster.com (for an estimated EFC that you can obtain ahead of time). Initially, you will record your adjusted gross income (AGI). If your family filed Form 1040, you can find this number on the last line of the front page of your income tax return. You'll also be asked questions about each parent's untaxed income. Untaxed income can be a number of items but is typically the amount you contribute voluntarily to programs at work, such as a 401k or 403b, that reduce your taxable earnings.

Both the FAFSA and FAFSA4caster.com will make deductions to your adjusted gross income. While you won't be asked to report expenses, a standard cost-of-living number will be subtracted from your family's adjusted gross income based on the size of your family. The larger your family, the greater the deduction will be. The amount you pay in federal, state, and FICA taxes is also subtracted from your income. A percentage of that income will then be used as the first variable that drives the EFC number. In Table 9.1, we show examples of EFC numbers based solely on parents' income.

The EFC numbers in this table are based on the following criteria:

- Family size: four
- Number of students in college: one
- Oldest parent: 47
- Student's income: $2,000
- Student's savings: $0
- Parents' savings: $20,000

Table 9.1: Sample EFC Numbers

Income	EFC Number
$40,000	1,443
$50,000	3,097
$60,000	5,038
$70,000	7,669
$80,000	11,056
$90,000	14,500
$100,000	17,727
$110,000	20,792

Parents' Assets

Assets are defined as savings and investments. You should report only the assets listed on the FAFSA. These include cash, savings, checking accounts, money market accounts, mutual funds, and individual stocks and bonds. You should not report the equity in your home or the value of retirement plans such as annuities, 401(k) plans, IRAs, Roth IRAs, or any other qualified plans. Don't report the value of life-insurance policies.

Every family receives an asset protection allowance on the FAFSA. Based on the oldest parent's age and the number of people in the family, some of these reportable assets will be protected. Beyond this allowance, 12 percent of the remaining reportable assets are used as the second element to drive the EFC number.

Student's Income and Assets

Each student is allowed to earn up to $6,000 that is not included in the calculations for his or her family's EFC. If your son or daughter earns more than this, 50 percent of these earnings are added to your EFC. If your child has money in a savings account, 20 percent of the total amount is added to the EFC. Note that custodial accounts such as 529 prepay tuition programs should be listed as parental assets.

CONCENTRATE ON AFFORDABLE OPTIONS

The other day I received an email from a parent who had attended one of my live seminars. I could tell from the email that she was struggling to understand some of the terminology. I encouraged her to call so I could clarify it for her. She did indeed follow up and contacted me via phone. The conversation allowed me to learn her story, a story extraordinarily common today.

Her first question related to the net price calculator of the college that her daughter wanted to attend. As soon as I heard these words "wanted to attend" my antenna went up. I suspected that the parent did not completely understand why and how she was about to misstep. The school her daughter wanted to attend was a flagship state-supported university out of her state.

"What did you learn when you completed that net price calculator?" I asked.

"Our net price was assessed to be $22,000," she responded.

Not knowing her family's financial position, I asked, "Is this an affordable amount for you?"

"Not even close!"

"Okay, then. Did you determine the net prices of colleges outside that category?" I was pleased when she indicated that she had. "What did you learn?"

"We learned that there were a number of colleges that had very low net prices. These colleges are in the highly selective private college and the traditional private college categories, but this isn't where she wants to go."

As I continued to converse with this parent, I learned that her EFC number was 7,000. A family with an EFC of 7,000 is of very modest means.

I explained to her that I thought she should encourage her daughter to focus only on college options that are affordable and disregard those that are not.

Her response was, "Well, I guess I don't understand then what this EFC is all about. If our EFC is 7,000, then why aren't my costs at each college $7,000? Isn't this what they calculated that I could pay?"

I explained that the EFC number is not what many families believe it to be. EFC is a number that determines a family's eligibility for programs, not necessarily the family's net price at each school.

She then explained that her daughter was a talented singer, and her top-choice college had invited her to a tryout to determine whether she would receive a merit scholarship for singing. The college would inform her of that in February. It was November of her senior year when this conversation occurred.

"Well, that puts you at a huge disadvantage if you place all of your time and energy on only one school and disregard other affordable options that might also have all the features and benefits that are important to your daughter," I explained.

I advised her to find out the maximum amount her daughter could receive in a music scholarship if she were offered one. "If the maximum gets the net price to your affordability threshold, then keep that school in the mix, not as the only option but as one option. However, if you find out that the school is still unaffordable if she receives the maximum scholarship, concentrate on other schools that are affordable."

Then she said what so many parents say: "My daughter will be incredibly disappointed. She has worked so hard, and she deserves to attend her first-choice school."

I explained that the situation with her daughter would initially be difficult, but that she had to disappoint her daughter now to keep her from having a lifetime of financial disaster.

Thankfully, she heard me loud and clear and began preparing herself for that very important family conversation.

The EFC Is Flawed

It is very important to understand that your EFC number is not the same as the affordability threshold that you calculated in Chapter 3. Your EFC number is not a good indicator of what you can afford to pay for college. As you have learned in this chapter, it may have been a good indicator in the past, but it clearly does not have the same meaning today. The main reason is that colleges do not uniformly meet 100 percent of a family's demonstrated "need," but there is another reason: the information used to calculate EFC is insufficient. The Department of Education has attempted to simplify the FAFSA over time. This simplification has led to less information being collected from families.

There is a movement taking place today to change the phrase "Expected Family Contribution" to "index number." This change would make the purpose of this number more clear to families, who would no longer confuse it with the cost of college. I agree that this change should be made.

A Comparison of Two Families

Before ending this chapter, I want to emphasize the point that EFC does not equal affordability. The following is a description of two families that have an EFC number of 14,000. However, when you read about their financial circumstances, you'll see that their affordability is quite different.

These examples go to show you why EFC is not a reliable number on which to determine your college affordability. This is why we included Worksheet 1, an affordability questionnaire, in Chapter 3 and a College Affordability Calculator at www.collegecountdown .com. This worksheet is designed to help families themselves accurately assess how much money they can afford to spend on college, rather than having someone else attempt to calculate it for them.

Both the Jones family and the Martin family have an adjusted gross income of $90,000. Both are families of four with one child about to enter college. Both parents in each household are employed, and the oldest parent in each is forty-seven years old. In both households, the student who is about to attend college earns less than $6,000 annually and has no savings. The parents in both households reported savings and investments of less than $30,000.

These are the variables that were used to determine that the Joneses and the Martins both have EFC numbers of 14,000. However, as you will see, many other financial factors should be considered when determining a family's affordability threshold.

- **The Jones Family.** Mr. and Mrs. Jones both have jobs that provide them with pension plans. They also inherited $250,000 when Mrs. Jones's mother passed away. They used this money to pay off all debts, including their mortgage, and placed $150,000 in an annuity to supplement their pension plans. The Joneses have a younger child who plans to attend a community college to pursue a vocational program. Therefore, the Jones' believe that they can use all their resources to help their older child attend college.

- **The Martin Family**. Mr. and Mrs. Martin have been employed in their current occupations for only a short time. Neither has a pension plan. They have a small IRA of $30,000 along with liquid savings. The Martins have $15,000 in credit card debt, two car loans that total $550 per month, and a mortgage payment, which they just refinanced for thirty years, of $2,000 per month.

As you can see, even though the Jones family and the Martin family have the same EFC number, they do not have the same affordability threshold for college. This is a great example of why you cannot rely on your EFC to determine your affordability, but instead should use the Financial Fit worksheets so you can make the best choice for your family's situation.

KEY POINTS

- Your family's eligibility for financial aid is determined when you file the FAFSA.
- EFC is a number your family receives when you file the FAFSA. In general, the lower your EFC number, the more financial aid your family is eligible for.
- The four primary variables used to calculate EFC are parents' income, parents' assets, student's income, and student's assets.

CHAPTER 10

DISCOVER MERIT SCHOLARSHIPS

Now that you have a good sense of your affordability threshold and how it relates to your EFC, it's time to look at options that may narrow the gap between your threshold and the net price of schools in which your child is interested. In some cases, where the gap between your affordability threshold and the school's net price isn't large, there are ways to close that gap.

Twenty-five or thirty years ago, there was little difference between the net price of college for a student with high SAT/ACT scores and outstanding grades and for a student with average test scores and good grades. Back then, students were primarily awarded money for college based on financial need. This type of assistance is called need-based grants. If each student's family had the same income and EFC number, the net price of college for the two students would be the same.

However, as college costs skyrocketed and resources from the federal and state governments leveled off or diminished, EFC no longer reflected what a family had to pay. The "need" was just too high, and many colleges did not have enough need-based grant money to make up the difference.

Many schools today try to make their net price more affordable by offering students merit awards, which are also called merit scholarships, merit aid, and merit money. Merit awards are not based on financial need. They are awarded for academics, athletics, or special talents.

The amount of money a student may receive in merit awards varies from student to student and from college to college. If a college really wants a student to attend, it may offer the student a substantial merit award. For example, suppose a college wants to increase the enrollment in its journalism department and an applicant has published articles in local newspapers while in high school and was editor of the school newspaper. The college will likely find this student highly desirable and may offer the student a merit award to ensure that its tuition is affordable.

According to *U.S. News and World Report,* 1,083 colleges and universities in the United States offered students merit awards for the 2009-2010 school year. About 14 percent of college students received merit awards for reasons other than athletics during that year. Merit awards and need-based awards are not mutually exclusive; students who qualify for need-based awards may receive both.

It's important to note that colleges within some categories are more likely to give merit awards than others. Most merit awards are granted by traditional private colleges, those in the traditional private schools and midsize private schools categories. (If you need to refresh your memory about college categories, turn back to Chapter 5.) Colleges and universities in the highly selective private schools category are the least likely to offer merit awards. These schools are more likely to fulfill the "need" by offering students need-based awards. Recently, more non-flagship state schools, especially those that are not in the student's state, have begun offering merit awards.

Merit awards can be grouped into these three categories:

- Academic scholarships
- Athletic scholarships
- Scholarships for other types of talent

Academic Scholarships

When most people hear the word "merit" relating to college scholarships, they think of academics. Academic scholarships are the most common type of merit award and may also be called presidential scholarships, deans' scholarships, founders' scholarships, or titles specific to a particular school. Two factors determine your child's eligibility for academic scholarships: his or her best composite ACT or SAT score and his GPA after six, seven, or eight semesters of high school. (Some colleges also request and include rank in class.)

Most colleges offering academic scholarships will offer the award as soon as they receive your child's application and high school transcript. (The scholarship is also later included in the official award letter your child receives from the college in March or April of his or her senior year.) Some colleges even include questions on their net price calculator that allow you to determine whether your child is eligible for an academic scholarship and how much money he or she might receive.

Other colleges don't make immediate academic awards but create a pool of qualified candidates. Students from this pool are invited to a scholarship competition program at the college. This competition might include some type of academic test. The college then determines the dollar amounts offered based on how the student scores in comparison to the other students invited to take the same test.

Colleges that award academic scholarships in this way typically do not include questions about academics in their net price calculators. Therefore, your actual net price might be much lower than the one indicated by the net price calculator if you learn after one of these competitions that your child has won an award. Consider a scholarship competition a future opportunity to lower a college's net price.

Note that colleges do not use a standard formula to determine whether a student is eligible for an academic scholarship or to determine the amount of the award. While some colleges might offer awards to students with SAT scores that are slightly above average, others might only offer awards to students with exceptional SAT scores and very high GPAs.

While some schools in all categories may offer academic scholarships, schools in these categories most often award them:

- Traditional private schools
- Midsize private schools
- Non–flagship state schools (out of state)

> # WHAT IF ACADEMIC SCHOLARSHIPS ARE NOT INCLUDED IN A COLLEGE'S NET PRICE CALCULATOR?
>
> Not all colleges include academic scholarship opportunities in their net price calculator. Make note of whether a school's net price calculator asks questions about academics when you create a category comparison table. Contact the admissions office of each college that does not include academics in its net price calculator, especially if a college is slightly out of your affordability range.
>
> Give the admissions officer your son or daughter's test scores and GPA, and ask if they translate into merit money. If they do, use the college's net price calculator again and subtract this amount of money. Doing this will help you determine whether a college is affordable and should remain on your list.

Athletic Scholarships

You have most likely heard about students who have received a full ride to college by playing a major revenue-producing sport, such as football or basketball. Perhaps your son or daughter is like these students and is talented enough to be sought out and recruited by coaches of sports teams and offered a full ride. This does happen, but it doesn't happen often.

More likely, your child plays a sport in high school and would like to continue doing so in college. Many young men and women who play sports at National College Athletic Association (NCAA) Division I and II schools and at National Association of Intercollegiate Athletics (NAIA) schools obtain some athletic scholarship money to lower the net price of college.

If your son or daughter wishes to play a sport in college and may be eligible for an athletic scholarship, discuss the situation with his or her high school coach, who can help you determine an appropriate level of play. (See the sidebar, "Divisions," on page 131.) Ask the coach to recommend colleges and give you some contacts.

If your son or daughter is not a "full-ride" athlete, you usually have to learn how to market his or her athletic talents directly to college coaches to receive some athletic scholarship money. Creating a resume that showcases your child's strengths will help you do this. Send this resume to college coaches at schools where the level of competition is most in line with your child's skills.

LEARN HOW TO APPROACH SCHOOLS ABOUT ATHLETIC SCHOLARSHIPS

Anthony Harrison played on his high school football team and wanted to play football in college. Anthony and his parents, Tony and Meredith, used Financial Fit and were disappointed to learn that most of the Financial Fit college categories were not affordable.

The traditional private schools category interested them the most, but it appeared to be unaffordable. Only the community college or commuting options seemed like they would work for the family.

They were hopeful that Anthony's desire to play college football might help their situation. They met with his high school coach and decided to focus on small colleges at the NAIA and NCAA Division II level. (Anthony's football abilities did not seem to be in line with those of Division I players. At the same time, the family's high EFC number kept them from receiving need-based money at the Division III level.)

Anthony created a resume highlighting his academic and football accomplishments. With the help of his coaches, he also created a video highlighting his skills. He and his parents made a list of thirty schools from the Division II and NAIA levels. They sent the resume and video to the football coaches at these schools.

Five college coaches responded and were interested in having Anthony on their team. Anthony eventually chose Saint Xavier University in Chicago. Using the net price calculator on Saint Xavier's website, the Harrisons estimated their net price at this school to be $22,000. After the college coach watched the video and spoke with Anthony's high school coach, Anthony received a $10,000 football scholarship, reducing his net price to $12,000 and making Saint Xavier an affordable option.

NCAA Eligibility Center

Be aware that your child must take specific core courses in high school—and do well in those courses—to be eligible to play at NCAA schools. Become acquainted with the NCAA Eligibility Center's website. The NCAA Eligibility Center certifies that registered athletes who wish to compete in Division I or II athletics programs have the required academic credentials and are amateur athletes.

Your child can register with the NCAA Eligibility Center by completing a student release form and an amateurism questionnaire during his or her junior year. Your child can view the course requirements after registration. Then he or she must have a copy of his or her ACT score or SAT scores sent to the center along with official high school transcripts. Becoming certified with the NCAA Eligibility Center is a requirement to be admitted to certain schools and to receive merit money.

DIVISIONS

Every school that belongs to the National College Athletic Association (NCAA) is in one of three divisions.

Division I schools must offer at least seven sports for men and seven for women, or six for men and eight for women. Division I schools must offer at least two team sports for men and two team sports for women. These schools must offer a certain number of athletic awards to students. They must play at least the minimum number of contests against Division I opponents and meet attendance requirements for basketball and football.

Division II schools must offer at least five sports for men and five for women, or four for men and six for women. They must offer at least two team sports for men and two team sports for women. Division II schools must have both male and female teams or participants for each sport's playing season and participate in at least the minimum number of contests for each sport. These schools must also meet attendance requirements.

Division III schools must offer at least five sports for men and five for women and offer two team sports for each gender. Division III schools must have both male and female teams or participants for each sport's playing season and have student athletes who do not receive athletic awards.

WHAT ABOUT CHEERLEADING?

Some schools now offer athletic scholarships for cheerleading. Your child will have to try out at a college to make the squad and determine scholarship eligibility. Be aware that the competition is fierce, especially at Division I schools. Scholarship recipients must be in outstanding physical condition, have excellent tumbling skills, and have an outgoing personality. You're not likely to find a cheer scholarship in a college's net price calculator. You have to contact the school and speak with admissions counselors to see if this opportunity is available. Some schools also offer small scholarships for school mascots.

Scholarships for Other Types of Talent

Some colleges offer merit awards to students who excel in areas other than academics and sports. The type of award offered varies greatly from college to college, so you need to check a college's website to see what opportunities are available for your child. (These scholarships often won't appear on a college's net price calculator.) You might find merit awards available for students who meet the following criteria:

- Students who live in a particular town or region
- Students who have attended a particular high school
- Students who have attended a parochial high school
- Minority students
- Students of a particular religion
- Students who have a parent who is a clergy member
- Those who have demonstrated outstanding community service and leadership
- Those who plan to major in a particular program
- Students who have a parent who is an alumnus of the school
- Students who have demonstrated artistic talents in the fine arts (theater, music, and art)

Tips to Help Your Child Obtain Merit Awards

We'll discuss how to maximize your child's benefits in detail in Chapter 13. However, the following are some tips to help your child obtain merit awards:

- Fill out the FAFSA: Even if your family's income is high, some colleges require filing the FAFSA even to be considered for a merit award.
- Look everywhere: Search college websites to see all the merit awards that school offers.
- Have your child apply to schools where he or she is in the top 25 percent academically; your child is most likely to receive merit awards at these schools.
- Ask about renewal terms. To keep some merit awards, students must maintain a certain GPA. Also ask about the number of years you are eligible for the award.
- Read and reread Chapter 13 of this book, "Maximize Benefits."

KEY POINTS

- Many schools try to make their net price more affordable by awarding merit awards, which are also called merit scholarships, merit aid, or merit money.
- Merit awards can be grouped into three categories: academic scholarships, athletic scholarships, and scholarships for other types of talent.
- To increase your child's odds of receiving merit awards, file the FAFSA and have him or her apply to schools where he or she is in the top 25 percent academically.

CHAPTER 11

LOCATE PRIVATE SCHOLARSHIPS

Finding and obtaining private scholarships is another way to lower the net price of college. As you know, a scholarship is free money, money that you do not have to pay back. Private scholarships can make certain colleges affordable.

Private scholarships are awarded by businesses, agencies, organizations, and clubs. Some of these scholarships might be familiar to you. You might know, for example, that the Lions Club and the Kiwanis Club offer scholarships to students in your area. The scope goes way beyond the Lions Club, though. More than one million organizations in the United States offer private scholarships.

Private scholarships are awarded to students who are outstanding in some way. These students may have exceptional academic achievement, leadership ability, participation in community service, athletic ability, or musical or theatrical ability. Private scholarships are sometimes also awarded to students who meet unusual but very defined criteria, such as scholarships for students who are left-handed or taller than six feet, two inches.

But while private scholarships are widely available, they are not easy to get. To capture the most private scholarships, you need to follow a smart approach.

The Problem with Scholarship Search Software Programs

To find private scholarships, many students today use scholarship search software programs offered by companies such as fastweb.com, scholarships.com, and cappex.com. To use these programs, students complete a personal profile. The software then matches the student's profile with the criteria needed to apply for each scholarship. Students then learn about dozens, hundreds, and, in some cases, thousands of scholarship opportunities.

Applying for so many scholarships takes a great deal of time. And because so many students use these programs and apply for these scholarships, the pool of applicants may be very large. This competitive pool makes obtaining a scholarship very difficult. While your child might use these programs to find national scholarships, he or she should first search for scholarships with a smaller pool of applicants.

The smartest thing you can do when applying for private scholarships is to start with the scholarships that have the least amount of competition, giving you the best chance of winning the award!

Four Categories of Private Scholarships

Independent scholarships can be grouped into these four categories, ordered by the amount of competition you'll have in trying to win the scholarship. You should search for them in this order:

1. Workplace scholarships
2. Local scholarships
3. Regional scholarships
4. National scholarships

Workplace Scholarships

Some companies offer scholarships to the children of employees. Check with your employer to see if this is an option for your child. If you're married, have your spouse do the same. If such a scholarship is available, make sure your child completes the application and submits it before the deadline.

Local Scholarships

Local scholarships are awarded by businesses, organizations, and clubs within your community and are often available only to students in your high school. All high schools have a system in place to make students aware of local scholarships. Have your child go to the guidance counselor and ask how the school informs students of local scholarships. (See the sidebar, "A System That Works," on page 139.) Knowing the process your school uses will put your child one step ahead of the game and help you make sure he or she doesn't miss important application deadlines.

Local scholarships typically offer your child the greatest chance for success because the pool of applicants is very small; in many cases, your child will compete only with his or her classmates. Have your child apply for all local scholarships for which he or she qualifies.

Regional Scholarships

Regional organizations also offer scholarships. Students awarded these scholarships may be from your county, city, or state. While the competitive pool for a regional scholarship is larger than one for a graduating senior from your child's high school, it is still small enough to give your child a decent chance at winning. You can often find regional scholarships listed on your high school guidance department's website under "Regional Scholarships" or "Area Scholarships." Check the websites of other local high schools as well.

SCHOLARSHIPS AVAILABLE THROUGH THE MILITARY

The military offers three types of scholarship opportunities. The first is through admission to one of the U.S. service academies, such as the U.S. Military Academy in West Point, New York. Admission to a service academy is a difficult, competitive process. You need a nomination from a member of the U.S. House of Representatives, a U.S. senator, or the Vice President.

You must have demonstrated outstanding academic performance, both in the classroom and on the ACT or SAT. You must also demonstrate strong moral character through participation in community service and leadership activities. And you must also make a commitment to that branch of the U.S. armed forces. The financial benefits of admission to a service academy are significant. The military not only provides free tuition and room and board but also a monthly stipend.

You can also receive a military scholarship by joining ROTC, the Reserve Officer Training Corps. Scholarships awarded by ROTC are usually based on merit, not need, and can be used at any school that offers ROTC in your particular branch of the armed services. After you graduate from college, you begin work as an officer in the armed services.

The third way you can receive funds from the military is to enlist in one of the armed services. An enlisted individual could receive tuition assistance for college while in the service or obtain benefits under the Montgomery GI Bill as a veteran. You can find additional information about scholarship opportunities on the website of each branch of the armed services: the Army, Navy, Marines, and Air Force.

National Scholarships

Lastly, have your child use the scholarship search programs we discussed earlier to locate national scholarships, especially if he or she has very high grades and test scores. Be aware, however, that these search programs are widely used. If your child applies for these scholarships, he or she could be competing with thousands of students across the country. While these search programs generate a large list of options, these options have large competitive pools.

The bottom line is this: obtaining a private scholarship is often difficult because many students apply. However, millions of private scholarship dollars are awarded each year. Your child has no chance of obtaining private scholarship money if he or she doesn't try.

How Private Scholarships Are Awarded

Once you win a scholarship, how do you get the money? Some organizations send a check for a scholarship directly to the student, while others mail it to the final college choice. Some colleges include private scholarships in their award letters. This policy might reduce other aspects of the award, such as the amount of money your child must obtain in student loans, but it may not reduce your net price. However, other colleges allow you to use private scholarships as a way to lower your net price, a much more attractive alternative.

A SYSTEM THAT WORKS

We developed a system at Hinsdale South High School, where I have worked as a guidance counselor for the past nineteen years, to make students aware of local scholarship opportunities. Like most high schools, our school is contacted each year by local organizations offering scholarships to our students.

Some of these organizations establish scholarship eligibility criteria and then ask our school administration to select the winners. Others depend on us to inform eligible students of their organizations' scholarships, and then members of the organization select the winners. In both cases, these scholarships are available only to seniors graduating from Hinsdale South High School.

Each summer before the start of a new academic year, we create a checklist listing each award and its requirement criteria, as well as the name of the sponsoring organization. We mail this checklist to all upcoming seniors, and we include their parents' names on the envelope as well. From my experience, parents are more interested than students in the financial aspects of attending colleges, so it is important that they are aware of local scholarship opportunities. Our checklist is reprinted in Table 11.1.

Our students review the checklist and check off those scholarships for which they qualify. For example, if an organization indicates that to qualify for its scholarship, you must be female, in athletics, and have a B or better GPA, then only students matching this criteria should check off this scholarship.

Students return the checklists to our guidance department in early September. We then compile students' information in a spreadsheet. We list each student's name and the scholarships he or she checked off on the checklist. Ultimately, this lets us know which students are eligible for which scholarships. Because these awards are only offered to students in our high school, all students who apply have a competitive chance at winning.

When scholarship applications arrive, we give one to each student who requested it. We also attach a cover sheet to make sure that the student is aware of all the requirements and accurately completes the application. In addition, we include a date when the student should return the completed application to our office. Most scholarship applications require a copy of the student's official transcript, so we request this from our registrar. We send the application and transcript to the organization before the scholarship application deadline.

Not every high school will follow this system to alert students of scholarships. Be sure to learn about the system your high school uses so your child has access to private scholarship opportunities.

Table 11.1: Sample Checklist of Local Scholarships

Please Complete and Return in the Enclosed Envelope by September 9.

Name		Student_Last_Name, Student_First_Name		ID	ID
#	✓	Award Name	Criteria		
1		Amanda Macal Memorial Award	Female, senior athlete, scholar, and citizen		
2		American Association of University Women	Female, top 10% of class		
3		Athletic Club Award	Parents members of Athletic Club, essay		
4		Jim Bonfield Memorial	Participates in Hinsdale South extracurricular activities, essay		
5		Booster Club	All seniors eligible to apply; essay required		
6		J. Kyle Braid	Seniors who applied for the J. Kyle Braid Camp		

Table 11.1: Sample Checklist of Local Scholarships, cont.

#	✓	Award Name	Criteria
7		Anne Coleman Scholarship	Darien resident; theater or music interest; top half of class
8		College of DuPage	Attending COD; rank in top 15%, ACT of 23 or 3.0 GPA
9		Community Bank of Willowbrook	Academic achievement, involved in activities; financial need
10		Darien Garden Club	Student interested in horticulture, environmental science, botany, ecological studies
11		Darien Women's Club	Resident of Darien; community service
12		Darien Youth Club	Participated in DYC four years or more
13		Garden Club of Hinsdale	Student interested in horticulture, environmental science, botany, ecological studies
14		Hinsdale Masonic Lodge	Male; financial need, high character
15		Hinsdale South Foundation/Steve Walton	Interest in teaching; essay
16		Hinsdale South Foundation/Jim Wheelock	Involvement in high school athletics as participant or fan; demonstrating enthusiasm for school
17		Hinsdale South Retired Teachers	Interest in teaching; essay
18		Hinsdale South Teachers' Association	Strong academics, extra-curriculars, and leadership

Table 11.1: Sample Checklist of Local Scholarships, cont.

#	✓	Award Name	Criteria
19		Hinsdale South Technical Ed	Portfolio required; participation in tech classes
20		Jennifer Darrow Memorial	Aspiring health-care professional; strong in science
21		Jostens	Essay required demonstrating need
22		Brian Taylor	Vocational or technical field; financial need, B average
23		Timberlake Homeowners	Member of Timberlake Association
24		Tzu Chi Scholarship	Financial need; B average or better
25		Carl Vuillaume Scholarship	Involvement in the theater program at South
26		Candace Wesolowski Scholarship	Active member of student body; B average or better; committed to drug- and alcohol-free lifestyle
27		Larry Labus Memorial Scholarship Willowbrook/Burr Ridge Chamber	Academic achievement; school and/or community service
28		Willowbrook/Burr Ridge Kiwanis	Key Club member, service; essay, letter of recommendation
29		Women's Club of Hinsdale	Female; top 5% in class

KEY POINTS

- Businesses, agencies, organizations, and clubs offer private college scholarships.
- Because many students use scholarship search software programs to locate private scholarships, the pool of applicants for these scholarships is very large.
- A better option is to pursue the four categories of private scholarships in this order: workplace scholarships, local scholarships, regional scholarships, national scholarships.

CHAPTER 12

COMPLETE THE FAFSA AND CSS PROFILE

The Free Application for Federal Student Aid (FAFSA) is the document used to determine your Expected Family Contribution (EFC). As we discussed earlier, the EFC is used to determine your child's eligibility for the federal grant program (the Pell Grant), the subsidized student loan program, and the federal work-study program. Some states also use the EFC to determine eligibility for a state grant, and some colleges use it to determine eligibility for need-based college grants. Filing the FAFSA will automatically qualify your child for the federal unsubsidized Direct Loan program.

Expect to see questions on the FAFSA about your income and assets (excluding retirement plans), your child's income and assets, the size of your household, and the number of children in your household who are in college.

You may submit the FAFSA on or after January 1 of your child's senior year of high school. The financial information you use to complete the FAFSA is based on the prior year, so you can't submit the FAFSA before January 1. For example, if your child will attend college during the 2013–2014 school year—from September 2013 to June 2014—you will use the financial information on your 2012 tax return to complete the FAFSA.

Because many families do not file their tax returns until March or April, you're allowed to complete the FAFSA using estimates from the previous year. In the instance above, you would make estimates using your 2011 tax return. However, if you choose to complete the

FAFSA using estimates, be aware that you must update your FAFSA information when your tax return is complete. More and more colleges are encouraging applicants to file the FAFSA early using estimates. A new federal data-retrieval service allows you to update your FAFSA electronically once you complete your tax return.

We recommend that you file your tax return as early as possible and complete the FAFSA with accurate information by the second week of February.

The way the FAFSA is worded makes it sound as though the student should complete the form. For example, one question on the FAFSA asks, "How many people are in your parents' household?" However, since you, the parent, are more aware of your family's finances than your son or daughter is, you will probably complete the form.

You can file the FAFSA online at www.fafsa.ed.gov or by clicking on the FAFSA link on the "Financial Aid Documents" page at www .collegecountdown.com. You can also download and print a PDF of the form and mail it. After you submit the FAFSA for your son or daughter's first year of college, you must submit a renewal for each additional year your child is in college. In other words, you must submit your financial information each year to receive a new award letter for that year.

Depending on the college your child wants to attend, you might have to submit a document called the CSS Profile in addition to the FAFSA. This form is much more detailed than the FAFSA and is typically required by schools in the highly selective private school category. Many Ivy League schools, including Harvard and Yale, require you to complete the CSS Profile. We'll discuss this document in more detail later in this chapter.

The FAFSA and Pell Grant Eligibility

When you submit the FAFSA, it is sent either electronically or in the mail to Federal Student Aid, an office of the U.S. Department of Education. The information you entered is used to determine your EFC number. If your EFC is 4,995 or lower, your child is eligible for a Pell Grant. You can see in Table 9.1 how income levels correlate to EFC numbers. If your EFC is zero, your child will qualify for the maximum Pell Grant, which was $5,550 for the 2012–2013 school year. If your EFC is above zero but below 4,995, your child qualifies for a Pell Grant but not the maximum amount allowable. The lower your EFC, the more money your child is eligible for in a Pell Grant.

Who Receives the Information on the FAFSA?

When you're completing the FAFSA, you must list which colleges you want results sent to. These schools will use this information, along with the information they obtained on the college application, to compose their official award letters. Colleges will not issue an award letter, however, unless your son or daughter has applied and been accepted.

The Student Aid Report (SAR)

After you file the FAFSA, you'll receive a Student Aid Report (SAR), which is a summary of your responses on the FAFSA. Check over the SAR carefully and, if necessary, make corrections. The colleges you selected on the FAFSA receive an electronic version of the SAR, called an ISAR. State agencies that award need-based aid also receive the ISAR.

If you provide an email address on the FAFSA, your SAR will be emailed to you within three to five business days. If you do not provide an email address on the FAFSA, your SAR will be mailed to you within three weeks. You can check the status of your FAFSA on this website (http.fafsa.gov) or by calling 1-800-4-FED-AID.

INDEPENDENT STUDENTS

The FAFSA requires both the parents' and student's financial information, unless the student is deemed to be independent. In this case, only the student's financial information is required to complete the FAFSA. However, students are very rarely deemed independent. To be considered independent from his or her parents, a student would have to be one of the following:

- A ward of the court
- Actively engaged in the military
- A veteran
- Twenty-four years old or older
- Married
- A parent who financially supports children
- Homeless or at risk of being homeless
- A graduate student instead of an undergraduate student

Your child also might be considered independent under some additional circumstances. If you feel that your child is independent, he or she should contact the financial aid office of each college he or she is considering attending. The college financial-aid office has the authority to allow your child to file as an independent, a process called a "dependency override."

Student Aid Programs Impacted by EFC Number

Your child's eligibility for federal student aid programs is determined largely by your EFC number. Do you remember this equation from Chapter 9, "Understand Expected Family Contribution (EFC) and Its Relationship to Financial Aid"?

$$\text{Cost of Attendance} - \text{EFC} = \text{Need}$$

As long as your EFC number is lower than your cost of attendance, a college may decide to include need-based student aid programs in its award letter. For example, suppose a student wants to attend a school with a sticker price of $25,000. His family's EFC number is 5,038. If you insert these numbers into the equation, you'll see that the EFC number is lower than the cost of attendance. This then creates the need.

$$\text{Cost of Attendance } (\$25{,}000) - \text{EFC } (5{,}038) = \text{Need } (\$19{,}962)$$

Eligibility for the following federal student-aid programs is often dependent upon EFC number:

- Pell Grants
- State grants
- Subsidized Direct Loans
- Perkins Loans
- Federal work-study jobs

Pell Grants

Unlike student loans, your child does not have to repay money awarded in grants. He or she also does not have to pay interest or fees to receive a grant. The federal government offers some students the Pell Grant, which is the largest college grant program in the country. In

2012–2013, the maximum amount of money awarded to each recipient of the Pell Grant was $5,500, but to receive this amount, a family had to have an EFC of zero. However, families with EFC numbers up to 4,995 typically receive some money in a Pell Grant. The lower a family's EFC, the more money it may receive through this grant.

Students may receive the Pell Grant for college for up to six years. However, their eligibility for a Pell Grant is determined each year, as is the amount of money they are awarded. Your child automatically applies for the Pell Grant when you file the FAFSA. In very rare, high-need cases, students will receive a supplement to the Pell Grant, called the Federal Supplemental Educational Opportunity Grant.

State Grants

Individual states may also offer grants based on financial need. Some states use your family's EFC number to determine eligibility. Your son or daughter may have to attend a college in your state to be eligible for state grant money. However, this college may be either public or private. There is no universally used cutoff on EFC numbers, but in most states offering state grants, your EFC has to be quite low.

Subsidized Direct Loans

As we discussed earlier in this book, Direct Loans are either subsidized or unsubsidized. The federal government pays the interest on a subsidized Direct Loan while the student is in college. The interest on a subsidized Direct Loan does not begin to accrue until six months after graduation. Congress adjusts the interest rate on subsidized Direct Loans every few years; in 2012, the interest rate was 3.4 percent.

All students are eligible for unsubsidized Direct Loans, regardless of their family's EFC number. The interest begins to accrue on an unsubsidized Direct Loan immediately. You can choose to pay the interest on that loan each month while your son or daughter is in college or you can choose not to pay this interest. If you don't pay the interest on the loan, the size of your child's debt after college is higher. This is called "capitalization." The current interest rate on an unsubsidized loan is 6.8 percent.

Perkins Loans

A family must have a low EFC number to be eligible to receive a Perkins Loan. These loans have a fixed interest rate of 5 percent and are subsidized, which means the government pays the interest on the loan while your child is in college.

The amount of money your child receives in a Perkins Loan depends on the particular college he or she wants to attend. The federal government gives each college a limited amount of money to award as Perkins Loans. Once this money has been awarded for a school year, it's gone. Colleges typically award these loans on a first-come, first-served basis and give them to the students with the greatest financial need.

You have to file the FAFSA to be eligible for a Perkins Loan. If you think your child might be eligible for a Perkins Loan, file the FAFSA as early as possible. Repayment begins nine months after graduation.

Federal Work-Study Jobs

Federal work-study jobs, also called college work-study jobs, are awarded based on financial need. To be eligible for a federal work-study job, a student must have a family EFC number that is lower than a school's cost of attendance, or sticker price. If you think your child might be eligible, answer "yes" to the question "Are you interested in being considered for work-study?" on the FAFSA.

Many students find jobs on campus that are not federal work-study jobs. These students are employed by the college as part-time employees. At many colleges and universities, you also have to file the FAFSA for your child to obtain part-time employment with the college.

FAFSA Sections Used to Determine EFC Number

The FAFSA is divided into sections, which are called steps on the form. Your responses to the questions in these steps are used to determine your EFC number:

- Student's income and assets
- Parents' income and assets

Student's Income

Your child is allowed to earn about $6,000 before his or her income impacts the EFC. If your child earns more than $6,000, 50 percent of the earnings above the $6,000 is added to your EFC number. For example, suppose Family A and Family B are nearly identical financially. Both families would have an EFC number of 10,000 if their child's income was under $6,000. However, Family B's child earned $7,000. This means Family B's EFC number is 10,500 because 50 percent of their child's earnings beyond $6,000, or $500, is added to the EFC.

Student's Assets

If your child has money in a savings account, 20 percent of it will be added into the calculations used to determine EFC. Any money designated in the child's name should be recorded as a student asset on the FAFSA. Of course, this does not include those assets that are not to be included, such as retirement plans.

A custodial account, like a 529 prepay tuition program or a UTMA account, lists the child as the owner and the parent or some other adult as the custodian. Note that if a custodial account is listed as a student asset, it produces a higher EFC number than if it is listed as a parent asset. Instructions on the FAFSA indicate that custodial accounts, especially 529 plans, should be listed as parent—rather than student—assets.

Parents' Income

Parents' income is the most significant financial variable used to determine the EFC number. According to the FAFSA, parents' income is initially your adjusted gross income (AGI).

Added to your AGI is untaxed income, which can be a number of items. Usually, however, it is the amount you contribute voluntarily to a program at work that reduces your taxable earnings, such as a 401(k) or 403(b) program.

Once parents' income is established, variables are applied to the income to reduce it. For example, the FAFSA does not ask you to report expenses, even though you most likely have them. However, every family is given an expense allowance based on the number of people in the household. The more people in your household, the greater your expense allowance. Your expense allowance is then subtracted from your income. The amount you pay in federal taxes, in state taxes, and to FICA is also subtracted from your income. The remaining income is the primary variable that determines your family's EFC number.

Parents' Assets

Note that while the FAFSA requests specific information about assets, it does not require you to report *all* assets. Reportable assets in cash, savings, and checking accounts are requested by one question. Other assets in CDs, mutual funds, individual stocks and bonds, commodities, and equity in real estate other than your home are requested by another question.

Every family is provided with an asset protection allowance based on the size of the family and the age of the oldest parent. Think of this as your emergency cash fund. Above this asset protection allowance, 12 percent of the remaining reportable savings and investments is used as the third variable to drive the EFC.

It is important to note that you should record the value of your savings and investments on the day that you file the FAFSA and not their value at the end of the previous tax year. Note also that you can do anything you wish with your savings and investments prior to the day you file the form, including positioning any assets in categories that would not have to be included on the document. These non–reportable categories are the equity on your home and the value of retirement plans, such as pension plans, IRAs, Roth IRAs, annuities, the cash value of life insurance, and qualified programs from your employer.

Which Parent's Information Should Be Used?

According to the guidelines for completing the FAFSA, a student's parents may be his or her biological parents, step-parents, or adoptive parents. A student's grandparents and legal guardians cannot be considered parents.

In a two-parent household, both parents' financial information should be included on the FAFSA, regardless of whether the parents file a single or joint tax return. If the parents are divorced, the parent and step-parent in the household where the child lives most of the time should complete the FAFSA. "Most of the time" can be defined as more than six months during the past year.

If a student lives with only one parent, that parent files the FAFSA. If a student lives with a biological parent and a step-parent, both parents' financial information should be included when filing. These rules apply regardless of who claims the child as a dependent on a tax return.

APPROACH FINANCIAL AID AGENCIES WITH CAUTION

Families often ask me if I do personal financial advising for college. I did this type of work for many years but then decided that I wanted to help more families than those I could visit with one-on-one, so I no longer do this.

I am always somewhat skeptical of advisors and planners who claim to help families find financial aid, especially when I hear stories like the one from a parent who called me in Fall 2010 after listening to one of my presentations.

She asked, "What do you think of the ___ Agency? They specialize in helping families find college aid."

I asked about the agency's fees and learned that while the cost varied, the top fee was $4,000, which this parent was contemplating spending.

I had a difficult time not displaying my displeasure over the phone, but I asked what the agency planned to do for that money. This parent told me that the agency was going to file the CSS Profile for her family.

My response: "I am completely confident that you could file the CSS Profile yourself without paying a fee. You might need some general assistance in understanding what differentiates the Profile from the FAFSA. And you might need some assistance in understanding how financial aid officers at colleges that typically use the CSS Profile think when they take those results and create an award letter. If you are convinced that you would like someone to file it for you, pay the agency $40. Helping someone file a CSS Profile does not warrant $4,000."

Then the parent indicated the real reason the firm could try to justify that charge: "They are going to reposition our assets so that we can qualify for aid."

The repositioning of assets is the heart and soul of the work done by many planners, and the concept necessitates a thorough explanation of good and effective financial planning for college versus planning that is exploitative and disingenuous.

An advisor or a planner doing competent work would first assess what a family could actually afford to pay for college. That assessment would also have to take into account their retirement goals and plans since most families describe these two financial issues as the ones they find most concerning.

According to the law, you must report certain types of savings and investments in filing documents to determine your family's EFC number. These savings and investments are liquid and include cash, savings, checking accounts, money market funds, CDs, mutual funds, individual stocks, and the equity of other real estate outside of your home. You should not report retirement accounts or the equity of your home.

You must report these assets at the time you complete the FAFSA. Because of this, you can alter the position of your assets prior to the time you complete the document.

After determining what a family can afford to spend on college, a good advisor or planner may examine the balance that the family possesses in savings and investments—specifically, the balance of liquid (reportable vehicles) with not-as-liquid (non-reportable vehicles) assets. Perhaps the balance is off and should be readjusted even if financial aid was not a factor. This type of advising can be effective. In some cases—but not nearly as many as portrayed by advisors—the movement of those assets could mean a lower net price at certain colleges.

However, in most cases, the movement of those assets doesn't translate into a lower net price. This is because assets do not significantly impact a family's EFC number in the way that income does. Simply stated, the system that determines EFC is primarily income driven and not asset driven.

If a family's assets are beyond the asset protection allowance, lowering the reportable assets will lower the EFC, but this will not necessarily lower the net price.

Sadly, some planners only focus on lowering a family's EFC number by repositioning assets. They then share the assumption with the parent that lowering the EFC will create a lower net price. Once again, this may or may not be true.

The good news is that this uncertainty can be eliminated with net price calculators. A family can input their assets—exactly as they are positioned now—into a college's net price calculator and learn the estimated net price at that school. Then the family can redo the process using the same calculator to remove the assets that they were considering repositioning and see if that significantly impacts net price.

If it does not, the family should only use an advisor to help them reach their financial goals after they correctly determine how college costs will impact those goals. The family should not use an advisor who tricks them into thinking that repositioning their assets will automatically make them eligible for assistance that they otherwise would not have received.

Now back to the parent who asked me the question—she should never pay $4,000 for a service that may have no benefit at all!

Repositioning Assets

While you can't change the adjusted gross income shown on your tax return, you can change your assets. You can do anything you like with your savings and investments. For example, you might choose to spend them on something you want or need. The obvious question then is this: Are you better off having fewer reportable assets while your child is in college when you must file FAFSA forms?

Certain assets are reportable on the FAFSA while others, such as the equity in your home, are not. Some financial planners charge fees to advise families to reposition their assets to lower their EFC number. While repositioning assets may lower a family's EFC number, it may not lower the net price of college for the family. (See the sidebar, "Approach Financial Aid Agencies with Caution," on page 154 for more detail.)

In many cases, families that hire a financial planner are not eligible for need-based programs based on their income. But the family's reportable assets have nothing to do with their ineligibility. Some financial advisors charge hundreds or thousands of dollars to reposition assets in an effort to lower a family's EFC when this has little to no effect on the family's net price.

However, if your income is relatively low but you have significant assets in reportable categories, then reorganizing those assets could lower your net price at certain schools. You don't need to hire a financial planner to test whether this is true. Use a net price calculator to see if repositioning your assets affects a college's estimated net price.

The CSS Profile

All colleges require you to file a FAFSA if you want your child to be considered for any type of financial aid, including Direct Loans. Some colleges also require families to complete a supplemental form called the CSS Profile. CSS stands for College Scholarship Service. The CSS Profile was created by the College Board, not the U.S. Department of Education. You can file the CSS Profile as early as October 1 of your child's senior year.

The CSS Profile is a more detailed questionnaire than the FAFSA and requires you to use financial information from your last two years' tax returns. The CSS Profile differs from the FAFSA in that it requires you to include the equity of your home and certain expenses that the FAFSA does not.

Only a small group of colleges require you to complete the CSS Profile, typically those from the highly selective private school category. Don't file a CSS Profile unless a college requires it; you have to pay a fee to file the profile and it's time-consuming to complete. The CSS Profile is used primarily by colleges that provide their own need-based money in award letters. Before these colleges offer this need-based money from their own endowments, they want to know more about your financial position than the FAFSA requires.

Colleges that require the CSS Profile most likely use the College Board's net price calculator, which is accurate and reliable. The estimated net price from this calculator should reflect your official net price if the information you provide is the same information that you list on a CSS Profile.

KEY POINTS

- You must file a FAFSA on or after January 1. Because many families do not file their tax return until March or April, you're allowed to complete the FAFSA using estimates from the previous year's tax return.
- After you file the FAFSA, you'll receive a Study Aid Report (SAR), which is a summary of your responses. You should check it carefully.
- Only some colleges require families to file the CSS Profile, particularly those in the highly selective private schools category. The CSS Profile is a more detailed questionnaire that gives colleges a more in-depth look at your financial history.
- Your EFC number is used, at least in part, to determine your child's eligibility for Pell Grants, state grants, subsidized Direct Loans, Perkins Loans, and federal work-study jobs.
- The sections on the FAFSA that are used to determine your EFC are student's income and assets and parents' income and assets.

CHAPTER 13

MAXIMIZE BENEFITS

Earlier in this book, we explained that you can use the net price calculator on a college's website to get an estimate of what that college will cost your family. But is it possible that the net price of your child's top-choice college could actually be *lower* than the price determined by its net price calculator? And, could one or more of the colleges that you initially thought were unaffordable actually become affordable? The answer to each of these questions is a resounding yes!

The key is to maximize your child's benefits. In other words, you need to make colleges aware of your child's strengths and talents and convince them to work with you to lower your net price. To do this, you should help your child create an outstanding resume and develop relationships with college admissions officers. You can even help your child reduce the net price of a college by appealing the financial determination made after you filed the FAFSA.

Use the Two Rs: Resume and Relationships

Many merit scholarships are awarded based on test scores and GPA, but colleges also award merit money for talent that is not strictly academic. Perhaps your daughter excels at debate and is a leader in student government, or maybe she has published short stories and served as editor of her school newspaper or spent countless hours volunteering at local charities. A college might find these talents highly desirable and offer your daughter merit money.

A college might even award merit money because it wants to increase the number of students majoring in a particular field. For example, a college known for its business program might want to bolster its liberal arts program, and thus students majoring in English or history might have an advantage at this school.

The first step in marketing your child's individual talents is to have him or her write a resume. The interests and accomplishments listed on your child's resume should include more than academics and after-school jobs. Your child's resume should reflect all of his or her talents.

Consider including the following on your child's resume. Keep in mind that you don't need to include all this information. Other than the heading and the education section, pick and choose the categories that best showcase your child.

- **Heading**—The name, address, telephone number, and email make up the heading, which should be centered at the top of the resume.
- **Objective**—The objective of a resume is its goal. Your child's objective might be something as simple as: "To obtain a scholarship as a political science major at Saint Joseph's University."
- **Education and Key Stats**—List the high school or schools that your child attended in this section, along with the month and year of his or her graduation. Include senior year classes and impressive classes taken in earlier years, such as AP classes. Key stats include your child's class rank, GPA, and standardized test scores.
- **School Activities**—List the activities your child participated in during each year of high school. Include clubs, sports, performing groups such as theater, and class activities. Be sure to highlight any leadership positions your child held, such as captain of the track team, president of the Key Club, or editor of the yearbook. You can also include "Leadership" as a separate heading.
- **School Honors and Awards**—List these along with the grade

during which they were received. For example, National Honor Society: 11, 12.

- **Athletics and Athletic Awards**—If your child is an athlete, list sports in this section, along with any awards received. Indicate the year or years your child participated in each sport. For example: Track: 10, 11, 12; Lettered: 10, 11, 12.

- **Community Service**—List any community service in which your child participated, along with the grade. For example, "Volunteered at Soup Kitchen: 11, 12" or "Soup Kitchen Volunteer: junior and senior years."

- **Work Experience**—Include part-time jobs and duties in this section. Include the employers, employment addresses, the dates your child worked there, and his or her duties.

- **Skills or Hobbies**—If your child is great with computers, mention this on the resume. If your child speaks a second language, this is a big plus. If he or she plays an instrument, be sure to mention this as well.

- **Other Sections**—It's fine to include other sections on a resume—whatever makes your child look good on paper. You might want to include headings such as Summer Programs, Foreign Travel, Special Talents, and Workshops.

While there isn't a standard format for college resumes, be consistent with whatever format you choose. For example, if you decide to use numerals to represent high school years, as in 11 and 12, do so throughout the entire resume. If you decide to spell out high school years, as in junior and senior, do this consistently.

The appearance of your child's resume is also important. Print the resume on good-quality paper. Be careful not to make the resume overly fancy. While it's acceptable to make the heading a larger point size than the rest of the resume, use only one point size for the body of the resume. Using 12-point is common because it's easy to read.

Make sure your child's resume is error free. Proofread it and have others proofread it as well. (For examples of college resumes, see Figures 13.1 and 13.2.)

Mark Ramirez
201 S. Main Street
Waltville, IL 60681
(708) 555-0198
markram@ezmail.com

High School

Academic Accomplishments
- **Student of the Quarter**
  - Junior year, third quarter, for U.S. history
- **Honor Roll**
  - Both semesters for freshman and sophomore years
- **Dean's List**
  - Both semesters for junior year
- **Increased GPA**
  - My GPA increased from a 4.41 in my freshman year to a 4.58.

Leadership Accomplishments
- **Boy Scouts**
  - Earned the Program Aide title, which allows me to watch and lead activities for younger children at camps and assist troop leaders with their troops and meetings.

- **Thespian Officer in Theater**
  - Maintained the title of Officer for two years.
  - My responsibilities are recruiting younger students to join theater and also taking part in each show. I also audition for the fall production and the spring musical.

School Activities
- **Freshman Year**
  - Theater and Drama Club
  - Art Club
  - Photography Club

- **Sophomore Year**
  - Theater and Drama Club
  - Art Club
  - Photography Club
  - Yearbook Staff

Figure 13.1: Sample College Resume 1

- **Junior Year**
  - Theater and Drama Club
  - Technical Theater Club
  - Inducted into the Thespian Officer Troop 878
  - Tom's One Day Without Shoes
    I assisted my friend in raising awareness of the more than one million children who are growing up without shoes. We hung posters throughout the school listing the diseases and infections caused by not wearing shoes. We encouraged students to buy a pair of Tom's shoes because for each pair purchased, a second pair was sent to a child in need.

- **Senior Year (in progress)**
  Current Involvement
  - Theater and Drama Club
  - Thespian Officer Troop 878
  Future Involvement
  - Technical Theater Club
  - Amnesty International
  - Tom's One Day Without Shoes

Community Activities

- **Library Volunteer Work**
- **Boy Scouts**
  - Volunteered at Camp Greenwood.
  - Participated in Polar Express.
    Assisted Troop 332 by reading to children, leading songs, and passing out candy while on a train.
- **Lantern Hikes**
  Our troop led hikes for more than 200 Boy Scouts ranging in age from 6 to 12 from one school to another, where we all gathered around a campfire and sang songs.
  Before each hike, we asked each troop to donate a bag of food that we gave to soup kitchens and families in need.

Figure 13.1: Sample College Resume 1, continued

Sandra Harrison
34 Mason Ave.
Apple Grove, IL 60627
(630) 555-0149
Sharrison3@ezmail.net

HIGH SCHOOL

ACADEMIC ACCOMPLISHMENTS
Freshman Year
    GPA 3.8
    Dean's List all four marking periods

Sophomore Year
    GPA 3.7
    Dean's List all four marking periods

Junior Year
    GPA 3.9
    Member of the National Honor Society
    Dean's List all four marking periods

Senior Year (in progress)
    Member of the National Honor Society
    ACT Composite Score: 30
    Dean's List

ATHLETIC ACCOMPLISHMENTS
Freshman Year
    Varsity Volleyball—Most Improved Award
    Varsity Basketball—Most Improved Award and Sportsmanship Award
    JV Badminton—First Seed Singles Conference Champion and MVP
    Presidential Fitness Award, two semesters

Sophomore Year
    Varsity Basketball—Team Captain
    Varsity Badminton—WSC All-Conference Athlete (Second Seed Singles)
    Presidential Fitness Award, two semesters

Junior Year
    Varsity Basketball—Team Captain and MVP
    Varsity Badminton—WSC All-Conference Athlete (Second Seed Singles)
    Presidential Fitness Award, two semesters

Senior Year (in progress)
    Varsity Basketball—Team Captain
    Varsity Badminton—Will play spring semester
    Presidential Fitness Award, first semester

Figure 13.2: Sample College Resume 2

You might also want to encourage your son or daughter to write in their college application essays about the experiences listed on the resume. For example, if your son was captain of the high school debate team, he should certainly write about how this experience enhanced his personal growth.

Once your child has created a resume highlighting his or her talents, you and your child are ready to work on the second R—relationships. While your child could simply mail the resume to a college's office of admissions and ask them to attach it to his or her application, this is not likely to generate the best results.

A better option is to have your child carry copies of the resume with him or her while attending college nights, visiting college campuses, and speaking with college admissions counselors. Have your child present the resume as he or she meets admissions counselors. The idea is to attempt to develop a relationship with a college admissions counselor in the hope that he or she can become an advocate for your son or daughter, matching your child's qualities to the merit opportunities at that school.

The initial meeting between your son or daughter and the admissions counselor is important. Encourage your child to introduce himself or herself to individual admissions counselors at high school college programs, and then express a desire to tap into merit scholarship options and give the admissions counselor a resume.

This is a sample introduction:

> "Hi. I'm Steve Jackson, a junior at Fairfield High School. I'm just beginning to explore college options. I'm interested in accounting, and I'm impressed with what I've learned about your accounting program. I've also been active in my high school and community. I would like to give you a copy of my resume so you can learn more about me. Whether I can afford your college is going to be a deciding factor for me, and I would appreciate anything *you* can do to help me find merit scholarship dollars."

Your child should develop a relationship with a specific admissions officer who will be his or her advocate. This admissions officer may take it upon himself or herself to find those merit scholarship dollars for your child. Admissions counselors often inform students of merit scholarship options when they give a presentation about their college. They might say something like this: "Our college participates in Division II athletics, which allows us to offer athletic scholarships in ten sports, five for men and five for women. We also have talent scholarships for artists, musicians, and students in theater."

Suppose your child plays volleyball and meets an admissions officer for a school he or she is interested in attending. After giving a presentation and meeting your child, the admissions officer may go back to her office and call the volleyball coach and say, "I met a unique kid at Fairfield this morning. I'm going to send you his information. You might want to send him an email or drop him a note." Developing relationships with college admissions officers will help your child receive merit money and lower the net price of college.

Consider Appealing FAFSA Results

Another way to maximize your benefits is to appeal the results of the FAFSA. After you file the FAFSA, you will receive an EFC number, which determines the amount of need-based money your child is eligible to receive to attend college. You can then appeal this determination.

The FAFSA is a snapshot of who you are financially. It includes your income from your previous tax return as well as your savings and investments at the time you file the form. This snapshot, however, might not give your complete financial picture. You may have expenses in addition to those requested on the FAFSA. Your financial situation may also have changed since you filed the FAFSA. Appeals are not heard by the federal government; they are handled individually through each college's financial aid office.

The following are reasons to appeal:

- **Loss of income**—If your future income or your child's future income will be lower than the income provided on the FAFSA, you should appeal.
- **Significant health care expense, including insurance premiums**—If your medical or health-related expenses are significant, you should appeal. The FAFSA does not request information about these types of expenses.
- **Educational costs other than for the student applicant**—You should appeal if you pay for other children's grade school or high school or if you pay for your own college costs.
- **Extraordinary circumstances**—If you have an usual debt situation or family issue, you should appeal.

A college might post an appeal form on its website. If it doesn't, compose an appeal letter such as this one:

Dear Financial Aid Administrator,

We recently completed our FAFSA and listed your college on the document. Soon you should receive our financial information and our EFC number. However, please take into account the following additional circumstances: [cite your circumstances].

The college will consider your request, and if it agrees with your appeal, it may then increase your award amounts.

Learn How to Negotiate Net Price

Can you negotiate a college's net price? Sure. Will a college admit that? No!

Suppose you were to ask a college's director of admissions and director of financial aid this question: "What do you dislike the most about helping families afford to send their son or daughter to your college?" They would most likely give you this response: "When they ask if we negotiate."

If you ask this question, they will say no—even though there is often room for negotiation. Try this approach instead: Do your homework and compile a list of net prices of three to five colleges with lower net prices. These colleges should be in the same category. For example, compare flagships with flagships, midsize private colleges with midsize private colleges, and so on. Then attempt to make an appointment with an admissions officer with whom you have established a relationship.

During the appointment, say something like the following:

> "My daughter Juanita has examined a number of colleges. We would really like her to go to your school because it is her number-one choice. We are trying to make it work financially but are falling a little short. We have also discovered similar colleges that appear to have net prices that are affordable to us. Is there anything we've missed? If there any other scholarship or grant that could get us where we need to be?"

If the person wants to see the comparison, be ready to show it to him or her. If this conversation takes place after the official award letters have been issued, show the admissions officer these letters.

If the admissions officer is eager to get your child to choose his school, he will often find a way to get the extra award money to close the gap between the school's net costs and that of its competitors. All it takes is some polite negotiation—just don't call it that!

Making the Most of Your Benefits

Remember that net price calculators are designed to provide you with estimated net prices of colleges. If you follow the methods in this chapter, you can possibly lower these net prices. Remember to have your child create a resume and foster relationships with admissions officers. You should also consider appealing the official award and learn how to approach colleges to see if they are willing to work with you to lower your net price.

KEY POINTS

- To increase your child's chances of receiving merit awards, help him or her create a resume showcasing talents and strengths.
- Your son or daughter is also more likely to receive merit awards if he or she develops relationships with college admissions counselors. Try to work with only one at each college.
- If your financial situation has changed since you filed the FAFSA or if you have additional expenses not requested on the FAFSA, you can appeal the results of the FAFSA.
- Even though college admissions officers say that they will not negotiate net price, they may be willing to work with you to lower your net price if you approach them in the right way.

Chapter 14
Analyze Award Letters

Receiving and analyzing award letters from colleges is one of the most important steps of Financial Fit. The official net price in the award letters is ultimately what will lead your son or daughter to select a college.

Colleges send official award letters to students in March or April of their senior year. Occasionally, a college will send a preliminary award letter based on limited information. Sometimes colleges send this type of award letter soon after your child sends in an application. Be aware that this is not an official award letter. An official award letter is received after the FAFSA and sometimes also the CSS Profile are filed.

The goal of a college award letter is to indicate and explain how the school arrived at your official net price. The problem is that colleges don't follow a standard format when they create award letters. While some award letters are very detailed, others are vague. For example, one school's award letter might break down the cost of each item included in its cost of attendance, such as the cost of tuition and fees, room and board, books and personal expenses, and travel expenses. Another school might simply list the direct costs, which only include tuition and fees, and room and board.

You have to determine which net price a college used so you can fairly compare award letters. Is the college using Net Price 1 or 2? As you can see, they are not the same.

Net Price 1

Cost of Attendance (Sticker Price) –
Grants and Scholarships = Net Price

Net Price 2

Cost of Attendance (Sticker Price) – Grants and Scholarships,
Student Loans, and Campus Employment = Net Price

Analyzing award letters is challenging because you have to make sure you're comparing "apples with apples" to fairly assess each school's net price. In this chapter, we'll discuss some common challenges you may face in analyzing award letters and some methods you can use to overcome these challenges.

Look Closely at Money Awarded in Campus Employment

Sometimes the amount of money offered in campus employment as a means to lower net price will vary from college to college. Consider this example:

College A	
Cost of attendance:	$37,000
Grants and scholarships:	$17,000
Direct loan:	$ 5,500
Campus employment:	$ 2,500
Net price of College A	**$12,000**

College B	
Cost of attendance:	$43,000
Grants and scholarships:	$22,000
Direct loan:	$ 5,500
Campus employment:	$ 4,000
Net price of College B	**$11,500**

College B is offering $1,500 more money in campus employment and, therefore, has a lower net price. However, not all schools pay students the same amount of money per hour for the work they do. Some schools, like College B, might list a substantial amount of money in campus employment but there may be little chance a student could work enough hours to earn it.

Therefore, to accurately compare the net price of College A and College B, you should eliminate campus employment from the comparison. You could also eliminate the Direct Loan, since this is a federal student loan and the maximum amount a student may borrow is the same at all schools. Now the comparison looks like this:

College A: Net Price without Direct Loan and Campus Employment	
Cost of attendance:	$37,000
Grants and scholarships:	$17,000
Net price of College A	**$20,000**

College B: Net Price without Direct Loan and Campus Employment	
Cost of attendance:	$43,000
Grants and scholarships:	$22,000
Net price of College B	**$21,000**

The net price of College A is now lower than that of College B.

Make Sure Cost of Attendance Includes All Items

As you learned earlier in this book, a school's cost of attendance is its sticker price. But what's included in cost of attendance? Cost of attendance includes tuition and fees, room and board, books and supplies, transportation, and personal expenses. However, some schools do not include all components that make up the cost of attendance. Some colleges include only direct costs—tuition and fees, and room and board—in their award letters but not the other items. Consider this example:

College C: Direct Costs, Not Cost of Attendance	
Direct costs	$22,000
Grants and scholarships	$3,000
Direct Loan	$5,500
Campus employment	$1,500
Net price of College C	**$12,000**

While College C appears to have a net price of $12,000, it lists direct costs and not cost of attendance. Direct costs do not include books, transportation, and personal expenses. If the cost of these items had been included, the net price of the school would be $4,000 higher. If you're unsure what is included in the costs listed on an award letter, call the school's financial aid office and ask.

Be Consistent in Your Comparisons

When you compare the net prices of schools based on their official award letters, make sure that you count all items included in the cost of attendance or include only direct costs. Be consistent. Either include a Direct Loan in all comparisons or omit this. The same is true for work-study jobs; either include them for all comparisons or do not include them for any.

When you compare the $5,500 in Direct Loans, determine if the ratio of subsidized and unsubsidized loans is the same. As you have read, the subsidized Direct Loan is much more attractive than the unsubsidized Direct Loan. You may choose not to accept the unsubsidized portion. (You'll learn more about educational loans in the next chapter, "Understand the Ten Loan Options.")

The Plus Loan Should Not Be Included

If a college includes a PLUS Loan in its award letter, the net price will look too good to be true—and it is!

PLUS is the Parent Loan to Undergraduate Students. It currently has an interest rate of 7.9 percent and is written in the parent's name instead of the student's name. The interest on the PLUS Loan accrues immediately, and most repayment programs begin immediately and continue for ten years.

The PLUS Loan should never be included as a financial aid element that reduces your net price. It is not financial aid, so you should not subtract it from a school's sticker price. It will make a school's net price appear very low, but in reality, if you're eligible for the PLUS loan, you can use it to pay for college at any school. You'll learn more about the PLUS loan and other educational loans in the next chapter.

Sample Award Letters

You can see sample award letters in Figures 14.1, 14.2, and 14.3. Keep in mind that if you were comparing these award letters, your goal would be to compare "apples to apples," meaning that you need to understand exactly what is included in each so you can make certain your comparison is accurate.

Look first at the award letter in Figure 14.1.

OFFICE OF FINANCIAL AID

2012-2013 AWARD NOTICE

Dear XX,

We are pleased to offer you the financial assistance described below for the 2012-2013 academic year while attending XX College. The award is based on the information you have provided to the Office of Financial Aid and is subject to revision if new information becomes available. Your financial aid is based on being enrolled full-time and living in campus housing for the year. If you DO NOT plan to live in campus housing, please contact the Office of Financial Aid as soon as possible.

Direct Cost of Tuition	$31,610.00
Direct Cost of Housing	$8,838.00
Financial Aid	$25,500.00
(Does not include federal work study)	
Unmet Direct Costs:	**$14,948.00**

Award Description	Fall 2012	Spring 2013
Presidential Scholarship	$10,000.00	$10,000.00
Unsubsidized Direct Loan	$2,750.00	$2,750.00
Totals	**$12,750.00**	**$12,750.00**

Grand Total:	**$25,500.00**

ACCEPT

DECLINE

You may accept your award online on the college's website using your User ID and Password or circle Accept or Decline and mail this form to our college's Financial Aid Office. All student loans (Perkins, Direct Subsidized and Unsubsidized) require an active Master Promissory Note and entrance counseling before funds will be disbursed to your account.

It is expected that you will have additional educational expenses such as books, transportation, and other personal costs while you are a student at XX College. These anticipated indirect expenses are not included in the estimated expenses found above. It is essential that you familiarize yourself with the information on the reverse side of this document. Additional information is available in the Financial Aid Guide. If you have any questions, please do not hesitate to call the Financial Aid Office.

Figure 14.1: An Award Letter from a Traditional Private College

This award letter is from a traditional private college. The college provides the estimated direct cost for the academic year 2012–2013. Note that the direct cost of tuition is given on one line and the direct cost of housing on another line. The total cost for tuition ($31,610) and room and board ($8,838) is $40,448. Direct cost may not include fees or expenses. This college is offering $20,000 in a presidential scholarship, which is gift aid from the college. Use this equation to determine the net price of this school:

$$\text{Direct Cost} - \text{Gift Aid} = \text{Net Price}$$

The net price of this school is $20,448.

Now, let's compare this award letter with the one in Figure 14.2.

FINANCIAL AID AWARD NOTICE

Dear XX,

Welcome to XX University. We are pleased to present your financial aid offer, which is based on your 2012-2013 Free Application for Federal Student Aid (FAFSA).

Factors used to determine your eligibility include Cost of Attendance (COA) and Expected Family Contribution (EFC). Your EFC, as determined by the FAFSA, is **$24,365.**

You estimated Cost of Attendance is **$44,754.** This includes tuition, fees, housing, food, books, and modest personal spending. Our university will bill you directly for tuition and fees and for room and board if you choose to live in the residence hall. We will not bill you for books, supplies, and personal items. If the financial aid you accept exceeds your expenses, you will receive a refund, which you should use to pay these other expenses.

Our policy is to offer you all the financial resources available to pay the full cost of attendance, so you may not need all the aid you are offered. If you have been offered loans that you don't need, you can reduce or decline them in eFinaid. See the reverse side of this letter for instructions on viewing, accepting, and declining your aid.

Awards are subject to revision based on funding, federal, state, and institutional regulations, changes in your enrollment or financial need, or the receipt of other awards.

Award	Fall	Spring	Total
Scholarships and Grants			
Non-Resident Tuition Grant	$9,908	$9,908	$19,816
Loans			
Fed Direct Sub. Loan	$287	$286	$573
Fed Direct Unsub. Loan	$2,464	$2,463	$4,926
Fed Parent Loan (PLUS)	$9,719	$9,719	$19,438
TOTAL	**$22,378**	**$22,376**	**$44,754**

Figure 14.2: An Award Letter from a
Flagship State University (Out of State)

This award letter is from a flagship state university that is out of state. This letter uses the phrase "cost of attendance" instead of "direct cost." Cost of attendance is sticker price, which usually includes tuition and fees, room and board, books, and personal expenses. Sticker price is cited as $44,754. This school is also giving gift aid, which it refers to as a non–resident tuition grant, of $19,816.

Comparing this award letter with the previous award letter is not easy. If you use the equation above, the net price of the school in Figure 14.2 appears to be $24,938. This appears to be higher than the net price of the first college. However, remember that direct cost and cost of attendance are not same. The second award letter includes money for expenses that the first does not.

There is also a slight difference in the type of student loans offered in these two award letters. The award letter in Figure 14.1 offers $5,500 in unsubsidized loans. As you know, this Direct Loan is available to all students regardless of income and assets. The award letter in Figure 14.2 also offers a Direct Loan, but $573 of this loan is subsidized, which is a better offer.

Neither of these award letters lists campus employment. However, students often are able to find some type of job on campus. To determine an actual net price, we recommend subtracting grants and scholarships, a $5,500 Direct Loan, and a $1,500 campus job from the sticker price.

Sticker Price − Grants and Scholarships − $5,500 Direct Loans − $1,500 Campus Job = Net Price

Also note one other element that's included in the second award letter, the PLUS. As we mentioned earlier, the PLUS should not be used to reduce your net price. The $19,438 PLUS on this award letter gives the false impression that financial aid is covering the remaining cost of this college.

Now let's look at the last letter.

FINANCIAL AID ELIGIBILITY NOTICE

Dear XX,

Thank you for applying for financial aid at XX University. We are pleased to offer you the awards listed below. Be sure to read the financial aid award messages and the financial aid terms and conditions enclosure. To utilize a student loan or work-study offer, you must accept these awards online or in writing. If not already listed, you must report additional financial aid you expect to receive such as private scholarships or university fee remissions. Carefully consider the loan aid offer and only borrow the amount you need.

ESTIMATED COST OF ATTENDANCE
Your costs are based on full-time enrollment on or off-campus.

Tuition and fees	$ 28,702
Room and board	$ 10,378
Books and supplies	$ 1,370
Transportation	$ 470
Miscellaneous	$ 1,560
Loan fees	$ 63
Total estimated cost:	**$ 42,543**

AWARDS

Federal Sub Direct Loan	$ 3,500
Fed Unsub Direct Loan	$ 2,000
Remaining net cost for family after student loans:	**$ 37,043**

Remaining cost can be met in a variety of ways. Parent PLUS loans and private loans are available to credit-worthy borrowers. Other options include our university payment plan or other financing options the family may have.

The information contained in this letter is subject to change as a result of action by federal and/or state governments, the trustees and the administration of the university. Questions concerning the contents of this letter should be directed to the Division of Financial Aid.

*Figure 14.3: A Second Award Letter from a
Flagship State University (Out of State)*

This award letter is also from a flagship state school that is out of state. This school breaks down what's included in its sticker price, which is helpful, but this school does not offer any gift aid. The only award included is a $3,500 subsidized Direct Loan and a $2,000 unsubsidized Direct Loan. This school's net price is shown in the equation below:

Sticker Price – Grants and Scholarships – $5,500 Direct Loans –
$1,500 Campus Job = Net Price

$42,543 – $0 – $5,500 Direct Loans ($3,500 Subsidized Direct Loan + $2,000 Unsubsidized Direct Loan) – $1,500 Campus Job = $35,543

So, which school has the lowest net price? It's either the first or second school. (The net price in example three is much higher than the others.) To be sure, you would have to find out what fees and expenses a student would have at the first school.

A Final Word about Award Letters

There is a movement taking place to try to force colleges to standardize what is included in their official award letters. We completely endorse this movement. Of course, not all colleges want to comply, as was the case with net price calculators. However, standardizing official award letters will help you to more easily find colleges that are a financial fit, colleges that you can afford without excessive borrowing.

KEY POINTS

In analyzing award letters, do the following to ensure that you are comparing "apples with apples":

- Use the same items to determine cost of attendance.
- Subtract only grants and scholarships from the cost of attendance to determine net price, and exclude Direct Loans and income earned through work-study jobs.

Chapter 15

Understand the Ten Loan Options

Once you have your official award letters and net prices, you need to determine what, if any, loans you will take out to help pay for college costs.

Taking out loans is okay; they are part of a prudent college financing approach. Very few students can afford to pay for college without some type of loan financing. Even students who receive grants, scholarships, and other types of aid may need to obtain student loans to cover the remaining cost of college. Remember, the key is to only take on loan debt that is reasonable, that stays within your affordability threshold, and that comes with the best terms possible.

Student loans are like any other type of loan—you or your child must pay back the money you borrow with interest. The lower the interest rate, the less expensive the student loan is. Federal student and parent loans *usually* offer lower interest rates and more flexible repayment plans than most consumer loans. However, always compare the interest rates and terms of these loans with those of other loan options. Loan options can be confusing, and as a parent, you should help your child make the best decisions about borrowing money for college.

Educational loans come in three categories: federal student loans, federal parent loans, and private loans. Let's take a look at the ten most common loan types.

1. Unsubsidized Direct Loans

Direct Loans are student loans that used to be called Stafford Loans. In the past, students received Direct Loans from banks and other financial institutions. However, since July 1, 2010, these loans are made through the Direct Loan program, which is funded by the U.S. Department of Education. Many college students rely on Direct Loans. In 2010–2011, 34 percent of undergraduate college students obtained Direct Loans.

Note that Direct Loans are student loans, not parent loans. They are written in your child's name, and your child will sign the promissory note. Your child must repay them. You do not have any legal responsibility to repay these loans. Additionally, your child does not need a credit history to receive Direct Loans.

Repayment on Direct Loans begins six months after your child graduates or drops below half-time enrollment status. If your child goes on to graduate school, he or she can defer repayment until after graduating with his or her advanced degree.

Direct Loans are either unsubsidized or subsidized. Unsubsidized Direct Loans are not based on need, so your child can get one regardless of your family's income and assets. The federal government does not pay the interest on an unsubsidized loan. Your child can either pay this interest while in school or add the interest to the principal of the loan and pay it after graduation. The best option is to pay the interest while in school so the amount borrowed doesn't grow. If your child borrowed $5,500 for his or her freshman year at the current interest rate of 6.8 percent, the monthly interest payment is only $25 per month.

Adding the interest to the principal is called "capitalizing the interest." Capitalizing the interest can increase your child's loan balance by 15 to 20 percent by the time he or she enters repayment. If at all possible, you or your child should pay the interest on an unsubsidized loan while your child is in college to avoid accumulating additional debt.

As soon as your family files the Free Application for Federal Student Aid (FAFSA), your child is eligible for an unsubsidized Direct Loan.

In March or April of his or her senior year, your child will receive award letters from the colleges he or she has applied to and been accepted by. A college's award letter will list its official net price. Most colleges will include the unsubsidized Direct Loan in their award letter to lower their net price. Your child does not have to obtain a Direct Loan listed in an award letter, but it is an option if needed. (Table 15.1 shows the maximum amount that a student may borrow in unsubsidized Direct Loans for each of his four years of undergraduate education.)

Table 15.1: Borrowing Limits for Unsubsidized Direct Loans	
College Year	Maximum Amount a Dependent Student Can Borrow
Freshman	$5,500
Sophomore	$6,500
Junior	$7,500
Senior	$7,500

2. Subsidized Direct Loans

Your child will only receive a subsidized Direct Loan if your family demonstrates financial need. As you learned earlier in this book, your family's financial need is determined when you file the FAFSA. With a subsidized loan, the government pays the interest on the loan while your child is in college. The interest rate on a subsidized loan is low, currently at a fixed rate of 3.4 percent. If your child is eligible for subsidized Direct Loans, he or she may still take unsubsidized Direct Loans up to the total maximum allotments for unsubsidized loans shown in Table 15.1.

Table 15.2 shows the maximum amount a student may receive in subsidized Direct Loans and the amount the same student may borrow in unsubsidized loans.

Table 15.2: Borrowing Limits for Subsidized and Unsubsidized Direct Loans

College Year	Max. Amount a Dependent Student Can Borrow in Subsidized Direct Loans	Max. Amount the Same Student Can Borrow in Unsubsidized Direct Loans
Freshman	$3,500	$2,000
Sophomore	$4,500	$2,000
Junior	$5,500	$2,000
Senior	$5,500	$2,000

Repayment Options for Direct Loans

You child has four main options for repaying unsubsidized and subsidized Direct Loans:

- The **standard repayment**, the most common type of repayment, is ten years.
- If your child accumulates more than $30,000 in student-loan debt, he or she can opt for an **extended repayment** from ten to thirty years. While extending the repayment lowers the monthly payment, it causes your child to have to pay more in interest over the course of the loan.
- **Income-based repayment** bases the amount of monthly payments on your child's discretionary income, which is defined as adjusted gross income (AGI) minus 10 percent of the poverty line for the family size.
- With **graduated repayment**, the payment is low at first and is increased every two years. The lowest payments are obtained through income-based and extended-repayment options.

Direct Loan Monthly Payments

Students who are eligible for the maximum subsidized Direct Loans and who do not take the unsubsidized portion of that loan borrow the following:

$3,500 during their freshmen year

$4,500 during their sophomore year

$5,500 during their junior year

$5,500 during their senior year

Total amount borrowed over four years = $19,000

At an interest rate of 3.4 percent, the repayment is $187 per month for ten years.

Students who add the maximum amount of unsubsidized loans to the maximum amount of subsidized loans borrow an extra $2,000 per year. If students pay the interest on the loans each month while in college, which is approximately $25 per month, they borrow and pay the following:

$5,500 in freshmen year

$6,500 in sophomore year

$7,500 in junior year

$7,500 in senior year

Total amount borrowed over four years = $27,000

At an interest rate of 3.4 percent for subsidized loans and 6.8 percent for unsubsidized loans, the repayment is $279 per month for ten years.

It is important to note that the maximum a student can borrow in Direct Loans is $31,000. The extra $4,000 can be used for students who need five years to complete their undergraduate education.

3. Perkins Loans

The Perkins Loan is a subsidized, need-based loan that currently has a fixed 5 percent interest rate. Undergraduate students may borrow up to $5,500 per year. To be considered for a Perkins Loan, you need to fill out the FAFSA. You should do this as early as possible because, as noted earlier, these loans are awarded on a first-come, first-served basis.

The federal government gives each college a limited amount of money to award as Perkins Loans. Once this money has been awarded for a school year, it's gone. A college's financial aid officers determine which students receive Perkins Loans. Typically, these students are those with the greatest financial need. Repayment on a Perkins Loan begins nine months after graduation.

STUDENT DEBT IN 2010

Two-thirds of college seniors graduated in 2010 with an average debt of $25,200, according to the Institute of College Access and Success's report *Student Debt and the Class of 2010*. Assuming an average interest rate of 6 percent, their 10-year repayment on that average debt is $280 per month.

4. Parent Loan to Undergraduate Students (PLUS)

Unlike Direct Loans, the Parent Loan to Undergraduate Students, more commonly known as the PLUS, is a federal parent loan. This means that the parent, not the child, is responsible for repayment.

PLUS is the most common parent loan. It is not based on financial need, and you can often borrow the full cost of tuition, minus any scholarships or financial aid your child receives. You can use a PLUS to pay for your child's room and board, books, and personal expenses. The interest rate on a PLUS is currently fixed at 7.9 percent, which is higher than the current fixed rate of an unsubsidized Direct Loan (6.8 percent). Since the PLUS is a parent loan, you should compare it against other loan options. Repayment on a PLUS typically begins immediately, not after your child graduates.

PLUS is the only type of federal education loan that takes credit history into account. Your credit scores won't be analyzed, but you'll be denied a PLUS if you have an adverse credit history. That means you have had a derogatory event in the last five years such as a bankruptcy, foreclosure, or tax lien. However, you can still get a PLUS with an adverse credit history if you have a co-signer.

5. Private Education Loans

Private education loans, also called alternative student loans, are offered by banks and other financial institutions, not the federal government. Private education loans are not based on need and are usually not subsidized. Many families accumulate excess debt through private education loans. Although many lenders offer private students loans, Sallie Mae, Discover, and Wells Fargo are some of the larger ones.

While private education loans are technically student loans, a parent must co-sign since a good credit history is a must. This means that if your child defaults on the loan, you're responsible for repaying it.

Most private education loans have variable interest rates that are adjusted monthly, quarterly, or annually. While these rates are low today, they may increase significantly over the course of the loan.

Obtaining a private education loan isn't always easy. You need a good credit rating: many institutions require at least 650 on a scale of 850, and some require higher than this. And even if your credit rating is good, you may be denied a private education loan. The institution may decide that you have a poor debt-to-service-to-income ratio. In other words, you have too much debt and too little income.

If you must take a private education loan, look for one that is aligned to the LIBOR (London Interbank Offer Rate) index. This variable rate index is based on the average interest paid in deposits of U.S. dollars in London. The prime lending rate, on the other hand, is a variable rate index that is the interest rate banks charge their best customers. The LIBOR index tends to increase more slowly than the prime lending rate.

Private education loans are definitely more expensive than federal loans. Use them only as a last resort. A better option is to use Financial Fit and choose an affordable college that doesn't require you to take out private loans. Keep in mind that a student with limited or no college debt is more likely to go on to graduate school. A student with excessive debt is more likely to encounter financial difficulties. Too much debt can cause your child to put off buying a home, getting married, and having children. Excessive college debt can even affect the opportunities of future generations.

STUDENT LOAN DEBT CAUSING INCREASED BANKRUPTCIES

Monthly student loan payments are forcing many Americans to claim bankruptcy. According to a report published by the National Association of Consumer Bankruptcy Attorneys, at least four out of five bankruptcy attorneys say that the number of clients they have seen with student-loan debt has increased significantly in recent years. And not just recent college graduates are in trouble. While the average college graduate has $25,250 in debt, the average parent owes $34,000, mainly in the form of PLUS loans.

6. Refinancing Your Mortgage

You may be able to refinance your current mortgage and borrow a lump sum beyond the mortgage payoff amount. You can then use this lump sum as a way to pay out-of-pocket college costs. This option is attractive because the interest rate you pay on any mortgage is fully tax deductible. If you have a significant amount of equity in your home, you can lower the interest rate on the loan. However, if you choose this option, make sure you can easily manage your new monthly mortgage payment.

7. Home Equity Loan

If you have equity in your home, you can take a home equity loan to pay for college. With this type of loan, your mortgage remains the same. The home equity loan is an additional loan in which the bank gives you a lump sum that you can use to pay for college.

This option makes sense if the interest rate on your mortgage is lower than the going rate today. Like a mortgage payment, the interest you pay on a home equity loan is tax deductible. You can also arrange for a longer repayment period than you usually can with a student loan.

Keep in mind, however, that making payments on your home equity loan should not extend into or interfere with your retirement. You must also be able to comfortably manage your monthly payments on your first mortgage, along with your home equity loan payments, or you could lose your home.

8. Line of Credit against Equity

Another option, if you have equity in your home, is to establish a home equity line of credit (HELOC) to pay for college. With this option, you don't actually borrow a lump sum. You write a check from the line of credit to pay the college when needed and only pay the lender interest, which may be tax deductible, while your child is in college. By paying only the interest, you keep costs on the loan down so you can effectively manage other college costs. Once your child graduates from college and these other costs have been paid, you can pay down the principal on the line of credit.

9. Borrowing from Retirement

If you have a 401(k), a 403(b), or another payroll-deduction retirement plan at work, you may be able to borrow money from this plan to pay for your child's college. If you do, you can often borrow up to half or $50,000 of the vested balance in this account, whichever is less. The interest rate on this type of loan is usually a point or two above the going rate. You will be obligated to repay your own account, principal and interest, over a five-year timeframe. If you are making contributions to this program, you may be able to reduce or eliminate new contributions to the program while your child is in college and classify these contributions as repayments.

Borrowing from a retirement plan can be attractive because it doesn't affect your cash flow. However, if your company matches a percentage of your contributions, don't go under that match with new contributions or you'll pass up free money. The interest rate on this loan is not tax deductible.

For example, Ray Samsell had a 401(k) plan at work valued at $300,000. He decided to borrow against this plan to pay for college. Ray had been contributing $500 per month into this 401(k) account. To help pay for his daughter's college, he decided to borrow $20,000 per year from this account, or $80,000. Ray actually made payments on this loan while his daughter was in college. He continued to have the $500 per month taken out of his paycheck but requested that it be classified as a loan repayment.

It is important to note that Ray's employer did not contribute to his 401(k). If his employer had matched his contribution, Ray would not have used his retirement plan to pay for college.

10. College Loan Programs

Sometimes, the college itself will give you or your child a loan to pay tuition. This is rare, however, and the interest rate and repayment options depend on the individual college.

LOAN CONSOLIDATION

Both federal and private educational loans may be consolidated—but not together. Your child may opt for a federal consolidation loan to consolidate Direct Loans and Perkins Loans into one payment. Consolidation might save your child money and may give him or her access to alternative repayment options. To consolidate private loans, your child can take a private consolidation loan. You can also consolidate PLUS loans. However, you cannot consolidate student and parent loans into one payment.

Accumulate Only Reasonable Debt for College

To protect your child's financial future (and yours!), don't take excessive loans to ensure that your child attends a particular school. This is an example of short-term satisfaction with long-term negative consequences.

Remember that $30,000 worth of college debt at 6 percent interest over ten years results in a $333 monthly payment; $40,000 of debt at the same interest rate over the same time results in a monthly payment of $444; and $50,000 results in a monthly payment of $555—and so on. While most students can manage a monthly payment of $300 to $350, they typically have trouble making payments higher than this.

A Final Word of Caution

People will tell you that educational debt is good debt because it leads to lifelong employment—and this is true to a point. Too much debt, however, can ruin your child's future and your future if you borrowed money to fund his or her college. Getting out of paying a student loan is nearly impossible. Student loans are almost never discharged during bankruptcy proceedings.

If your child defaults on a student loan, the federal government can garnish up to 15 percent of his or her wages and confiscate tax-refund checks. The government will even confiscate lottery winnings if your child defaults on a student loan! Defaulting on a student loan will make it difficult for your child to get a mortgage, a car loan, or a credit card. Since a credit report is often required to rent an apartment, your child may not even be able to leave home.

Remember that just because a loan is available is not a good reason to take it. You should always make sure to stay within your affordability threshold and seek the loans with the best terms possible.

KEY POINTS

- Educational loans come in three categories: federal student loans, federal parent loans, and private loans.
- Direct Loans are federal student loans, not parent loans. This means that, as a parent, you have no legal reason to repay these loans.
- While subsidized Direct Loans are based on need, unsubsidized Direct Loans are not. As soon as you file the FAFSA, your child is eligible for unsubsidized Direct Loans.
- A PLUS (Parent Loan for Undergraduate Students) is a federal parent loan not based on need.
- Private educational loans are offered by banks and other financial institutions. They are not subsidized or based on need.

CHAPTER 16

CHOOSE THE RIGHT COLLEGE AT THE RIGHT PRICE

A t this point, you have made your way through most of the steps in the Execution Phase of Financial Fit.

- You have located private scholarships and merit scholarships that could help to lower the net price of college.
- You have completed and filed the FAFSA and possibly the CSS Profile, depending on the schools on your child's list.
- You helped your child create a resume and establish relationships with college admissions officers to maximize your child's benefits.
- Your son or daughter has received award letters from the colleges on his or her list.
- You have analyzed these award letters to ensure that you're comparing "apples with apples" so that your official net price comparison is fair.
- You have considered the ten loan options in order to pay for school without excessive borrowing.

Now, it's time for the last step in Financial Fit—choosing the right college.

Forget about Net Price

Throughout this book, we've stressed the importance of choosing a school that is affordable for your family. However, at this late stage in the process, the four to six schools on your child's list should have net prices that are affordable or very close to being affordable. At this time, you should forget about net price and have your child rank the schools according to his or her preferences.

This is important because you then know which schools are your child's top choices. This gives you a foundation to work from if you want to try to correct net price differences using the techniques from the previous chapters.

The following case study is a great example of why this is the best approach.

Case Study: Margaret Montelo

Margaret Montelo and her parents had progressed through the steps in the Execution Phase of the Financial Fit program and were ready to select a school. These schools remained on Margaret's list:

- Kalamazoo College (Kalamazoo, Michigan)
- DePauw University (Greencastle, Indiana)
- Denison University (Granville, Ohio)
- Cornell College (Mount Vernon, Iowa)

Margaret's preferences were to attend a small college in a small town or city with a strong liberal arts program and a nurturing campus environment. Margaret hoped the school she chose would have a tennis team so she could play tennis, but this was not essential. Margaret also planned to try out for school plays. She was going to major in English and wanted to one day attend law school.

Margaret and her family visited each of these schools during her senior year. They learned through Financial Fit that these schools were likely to all be affordable.

Margaret ranked the schools on her list as if they all had the same net price:

1. Cornell College
2. DePauw University

3. Denison University
4. Kalamazoo College

The Montelos' affordability threshold was $28,000, a fairly high amount. This was good news for Margaret because only a few of the Financial Fit college categories were unaffordable for her family. However, the $28,000 was the most the Montelos could afford to spend on college each year. These were the net prices of the colleges on Margaret's list:

1. Cornell College $32,000
2. DePauw University $33,000
3. Denison University $28,000
4. Kalamazoo College $27,000

Based on these prices, Margaret could attend Denison or Kalamazoo—and these schools matched her preferences. However, the Montelos decided to visit Cornell College once more before making a final choice.

The Montelos scheduled a meeting with the admissions officer whom they had worked with all year. They told her that they needed to meet with someone who was in a position to help them make their final college choice because they had several attractive options to choose from.

Note that Margaret and her parents did not ask the admissions officer, "Do you negotiate?" If they did, the admissions officer would have undoubtedly answered, "No!" While you should never ask college officials if they negotiate, the reality is that many colleges are willing to work with you on net price if they believe that your child sincerely wants to attend their school.

The admissions officer arranged a meeting for the Montelos with the dean of enrollment. The Montelos showed the dean the award letters from the other colleges on Margaret's list. They also showed the dean the worksheet they used to determine their affordability threshold. Ms. Montelo then said, "Margaret likes all of her college options but Cornell College is clearly her number-one choice. We would like her to attend your school, but we simply cannot pay more than $28,000 per year. Are there any other programs that we may have missed that might lower our net price?"

The ball was now in the hands of the dean. When you ask a college official if the college has additional programs that might lower your net price, some college officials will tell you, "No. There is nothing else that we can do." However, other college officials will find another resource to make their school affordable for your family.

The dean at Cornell did find a way to increase Margaret's award money, making her top choice now affordable for her.

If Margaret had not ranked her choices before looking at the net prices, the Montelos may not have known or been as inclined to try to negotiate the net price at Cornell to make that option work for them. They would have had to make a quick decision to choose one of the other schools. But with the knowledge in hand that Cornell was Margaret's top choice, they were then able to review the net price differences in the best light and maximize Margaret's benefits so her final choice got her entrance into the right college at the right price.

The Right College at the Right Price

So now it's decision time. Everything we've discussed so far in this book boils down to choosing the right college for you at the right price. So before we move on, it's important to say a few words about what makes a school the right college at the right price.

Unfortunately, there is a lot of misinformation that confuses the issue of what makes a "right college" for you.

Many colleges today support the return-on-investment (ROI) theory, which suggests that any college is worth the cost. Much research clearly supports this theory. College graduates earn substantially more during their lifetime than those who completed only high school. (See Figure 16.1.) But is any college really worth the cost, no matter how much debt you accumulate along the way? What you've learned in this book clearly says no.

Some colleges take this theory a step further and suggest that an undergraduate education at their school is worth more than at other schools, thus making people more inclined to take on excessive debt to attend those schools. The many magazines that rank colleges also advocate the idea that some schools are better than others. However, a student's ROI may have more to do with the student than with the school he or she attends, according to a study by economists Stacy Dale and Alan Krueger.

After more than a decade of research, Dale and Krueger published research indicating that elite colleges, those in the highly selective private schools category, did appear to have more graduates that generate higher earnings over the course of their working life. However, while many students who graduate from elite schools earn more than those who graduate from other schools, Dale and Krueger contend that this may have more to do with the students than the schools. They point out that students who apply to these schools are often extremely confident and ambitious, which likely leads them to work harder than others. Krueger's advice to students was published in the *New York Times*:

> "Don't believe that the only school worth attending is one that would not admit you. That you go to college is more important than where you go. Find a school whose academic strengths match your interests and that devotes resources to instruction in those fields. Recognize that your own motivation, ambition, and talents will determine your success more than the college name on your diploma."

Therefore, you shouldn't decide to attend any college regardless of the cost. And you shouldn't take on excessive debt to attend a college that's "ranked" higher than one that's affordable for you, since your own efforts matter more to your success that the prestige of the school you attend.

So what is the right college for you? Choosing the right college at the right price combines every aspect that you learned from the start of the planning phase of the college selection process through the very last conversation you have with an admissions officer during the execution phase. The right college fits your child academically, personally, culturally, and socially. Most of all, the right college fits your family financially so that you and your child can pay for college without excessive debt. By finding a school that achieves both, you will have the right college at the right price. And that is one of the best decisions you can ever make.

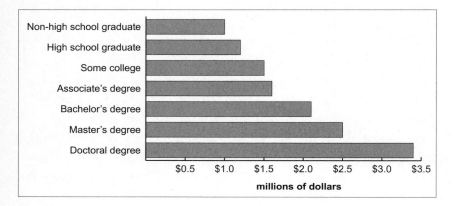

Figure 16.1: Work-Life Earnings Estimates for Full-Time, Year-Round Workers by Educational Attainment

KEY POINTS

- When you're at the very end of the college search process and have several schools that are affordable for your family, have your child forget about net price and rank the schools according to his or her preferences.
- If your child's first choice is slightly above your affordability threshold, arrange a meeting with college officials to see if they can work with you to lower the net price.
- While some colleges claim students get a better return on investment (ROI) at their school, the truth is that ROI depends more on the student than the school.

CHAPTER 17

MANAGE COSTS EFFECTIVELY WHILE IN COLLEGE

The goal of Financial Fit is to help you and your child avoid making the mistake that so many families make today—accumulating too much debt to pay for college. Our method teaches you to find multiple affordable college options and to use the information you obtain as leverage to ensure that you receive the best possible net price.

However, that doesn't end once your child has been admitted to his or her right college. You need to keep up the good work while your child is in college and effectively manage college expenses. Here are some of the most effective ways to stay financially fit all through the college years.

Try to Lock in Your Net Price

When your child receives an official award letter and is ready to make a final decision about attending a school, ask college officials about locking in the awards that are under the college's control. Note that federal and state grant awards are not under the college's control. Your child's eligibility for these awards is determined each year when you file the FAFSA renewal form. However, the college can control what it offers in institution awards, which are scholarships and need-based college grants.

Chances are the college's costs will increase each year. Ask college officials if they are willing to increase your child's scholarship or grant, or both, to compensate for those increases. Explain that while you can afford their net price this year, it may become unaffordable if it increases in subsequent years.

Colleges care about their retention rates. They do not want to lose students once they are enrolled. College officials may work with you to ensure that your first-year net price does not increase significantly over the next three years.

Finish in Four Years

While some undergraduate programs take five or six years to complete, most do not. Yet many college students today take longer than four years to complete an undergraduate degree. The U.S. Department of Education reports that 45 percent of college students take five or more years to complete a bachelor's degree. On some college campuses, nearly all students need an extra year or two.

Why? It is not because students attend school part-time or leave for a year or two and then return. It is usually because of poor planning. Procrastination is often to blame. Students put off meeting with advisors and registering for classes. When they do finally register, the classes they need to take are filled. Other students take too many difficult classes in one semester and wind up dropping a class or two. Students who switch majors often need five or six years to graduate. Focusing too much on socializing instead of studying is another reason for the extra year or two.

Discuss with your child the importance of finishing on time. Taking five or six years to complete an undergraduate degree significantly increases the net price of college and possibly the amount of debt your child accumulates. College costs are too high to make this mistake.

Your child may also lose out on earnings from a year of employment by taking an extra year. He or she could have been working full-time instead of remaining in school. Stress that taking five or six years to complete a bachelor's degree does not look good on a resume.

Help your child graduate on time by helping him or her balance difficult classes with easier ones each semester to avoid having to drop a class. Have your child meet with advisors and register for classes as early as possible. Stress the importance of taking the time to learn about a major before choosing it. Talk to people in the field and college advisors. Once your child chooses a major, encourage him or her to stick with it.

It is also imperative that you, the parent, communicate with college advisors to be certain that the academic path your child is on will lead to a degree in four years. If you don't pay attention to your child's progress each semester, the fifth year can blindside you. Most families are not prepared to handle this extra cost.

Consider Graduating in Three Years

Industrious students who take the maximum number of allowable credits each semester may be able to graduate in three years. This is especially true for students who have advance placement credits from courses taken in high school.

Graduating in three years instead of four can save your family a great deal of money. Your child may attend a college with a standard annual tuition rate that remains the same whether a student completes fifteen or eighteen credits per semester. In this case, your child can essentially take an extra class for free.

Become a Resident Assistant (RA)

A resident assistant (RA), sometimes called a resident advisor, is a college student employed by the college to help supervise and manage a floor of a dormitory. While some RAs are sophomores, many are upperclassmen who have lived in a dormitory at least a year. If your child becomes a resident assistant (RA), your family could save $8,000 to $10,000 per year in college costs. Many colleges offer RAs free room and board along with a stipend.

It is not easy to become an RA. Colleges want mature students who can handle the responsibility of supervising students living on a floor in a dormitory, organizing activities, and disciplining students who have broken the rules. If you think your child is capable of handling this responsibility, encourage him or her to learn how to apply for this position. In addition to saving thousands of dollars in college costs, past experience as an RA looks great on a resume because it shows that your child has leadership and conflict-management skills.

Be Smart in Purchasing Books

When purchased new, college textbooks are extremely expensive. The average college student spends about $1,122 on textbooks. Be on the lookout for ways to save money on books.

Begin by comparison shopping. Search for used copies of books online. Try searching for used textbooks on websites such as www.campusbooks.com. Consider buying an older edition of a book being used for a class. Often the changes from one edition to the next are extremely minor. However, to be sure that this is the case, have your child ask his or her professor if the older edition of a textbook is acceptable.

Also consider renting textbooks. If your child's school campus bookstore does not allow students to rent textbooks, look into textbook rental services online. Also check if a hard-copy edition of a book is available online for ebook readers, such as Kindle.

Have your child shop for textbooks before school starts. Because of a new federal law, students must receive a list of required textbooks during registration. Your child will find better bargains if he or she begins looking before the start of the semester. If you are paying part or all of the net price of college for your child, have him or her work during the summer to pay for books.

Take Summer Courses at a Community College

Your child's school may allow students to take at least some courses at a community college. If this is the case, have your child take advantage and complete some coursework at a community college during the summer. A course at a community college costs only a fraction of one at a private college or university, so you may be able to save thousands of dollars. However, have your child check with an academic advisor before taking any course at a community college to make sure that the course fits into his or her program of study and will be accepted.

Begin Thinking Early about Life after Graduation

Too many college students start to consider what they will do after graduation during the second semester of their senior year. Encourage your child to begin thinking about the next step as early as possible. Have your child consult the career planning and placement office. He or she should pursue internships, learn how to ace a job interview, and create a resume. If your child does not plan to attend graduate school, he or she should concentrate on landing a job as soon as possible after graduation. While setting goals in college won't lower your child's annual net price, it may help him or her start earning money sooner after graduation.

Consider the Price of Graduate School

If your son or daughter is in an academic discipline that will lead to a graduate or professional school, look for a school with an affordable net price. A graduate course typically costs more than an undergraduate course, but graduate students have unique opportunities to cover some or all of the cost of attendance.

Many graduate programs offer merit scholarships and fellowships that cover at least part of the tuition. These awards are given by individual departments and not the financial aid office, so your child should contact the department chairperson to learn how to apply. Graduate schools also offer research and teaching assistantships, some of which cover the entire cost of tuition and pay a stipend for time spent on research or classroom instruction.

Your child needs to file the FAFSA to see if he or she is eligible for federal loans such as the Perkins Loan for graduate school. Students may also obtain Direct Loans for graduate school, and parents may obtain Graduate PLUS loans.

LEARN TO CONTROL COSTS TO PREPARE FOR GRADUATE OR PROFESSIONAL SCHOOL

In 1995, Mr. Chaudhury called to ask me to speak to his son T.J., who was an exceptionally bright student with a host of academic accomplishments at our high school. T.J. was thrilled when he received a letter of acceptance from prestigious Duke University. However, the offer in the award letter was not nearly what the Chaudhury family needed to send T.J. to Duke. In fact, if T.J. attended Duke, either T.J. or his parents would have to borrow so much money that they would be in financial jeopardy.

Young people have difficulty grasping financial situations and discussing finances with their parents because they have a hard time seeing the long-term big picture. T.J. was no exception. The lure of the experience he would have at Duke permeated his thinking.

This is why Mr. Chaudhury asked me to speak to his son. He explained that T.J. had another college opportunity—and an unusual and extraordinary one at that. Benedictine University had offered T.J. a full scholarship. Benedictine is a small college noted for its strong undergraduate science program and for the number of alumni who continue on to medical school, something T.J. planned to do.

Mr. Chaudhury believed that T.J. might have the experience of his life at Duke but could end up with a student debt burden that would be difficult to manage. Since T.J. planned to attend medical school, his future debt burden could be quite high. At Benedictine, T.J. could receive a high-quality undergraduate education for no cost and conserve his resources for medical school.

I spoke with T.J. and he decided to attend Benedictine. However, I always felt that he reluctantly acquiesced to his family's wishes and perhaps even to mine.

I didn't know how the story played out until 2009 when the secretary in our school counseling office asked if I would take a call from a Dr. Chaudhury. She said he indicated that he wanted to know how to establish a scholarship for the school. As the scholarship coordinator, I frequently receive these types of calls.

I accepted the call and recognized the last name. "Is this T.J.?" I asked.

"Mr. Palmasani," he replied, "I didn't know if you would remember me."

"I sure do," I said. "Do you remember our conversation?"

"Absolutely," he replied.

"What ended up happening?"

"I went to Benedictine and then on to medical school. Benedictine was a fantastic experience. I received a great education, and my family was able to handle the expense of medical school. I really appreciate that conversation."

Even in 1995, college costs were an issue for families. Although not many students are offered a full scholarship, students and parents can enhance their opportunity to find affordable college options by following the principles of Financial Fit.

KEY POINTS

- To keep the cost of college under control, insist that your child earn a bachelor's degree in four years, and not in five or six years as many students today do.
- Your child can earn $8,000 to $10,000 per year for college, along with free room and board, by working as a resident assistant (RA).
- Work with college officials to keep your net price the same as college costs increase each year.
- In buying college textbooks, look for the most inexpensive options.
- To lower the cost of college, your child should consider taking summer courses at a community college.
- Graduating in three years instead of four is another way to reduce the cost of college.

APPENDIX

Flagship State Schools

Alabama
Auburn University
University of Alabama

Arizona
Arizona State University
University of Arizona

Arkansas
University of Arkansas

California
University of California Berkeley

Colorado
University of Colorado Boulder

Connecticut
University of Connecticut

Delaware
University of Delaware

Florida
University of Florida

Georgia
University of Georgia

Hawaii
University of Hawaii

Idaho
University of Idaho

Illinois
University of Illinois at Urbana-Champaign

Indiana
Indiana University Bloomington
Purdue University

Iowa
University of Iowa

Kansas
University of Kansas

Kentucky
University of Kentucky
University of Louisville

Louisiana
Louisiana State University

Maine
University of Maine

Maryland
University of Maryland

Massachusetts
University of Massachusetts

Michigan
Michigan State University
University of Michigan

Minnesota
University of Minnesota

Mississippi
University of Mississippi

Missouri
University of Missouri–Columbia

Montana
University of Montana

Nebraska
University of Nebraska

Nevada
University of Nevada, Las Vegas (UNLV)

New Hampshire
University of New Hampshire

New Jersey
Rutgers University

New Mexico
University of New Mexico

North Carolina
North Carolina State University
University of North Carolina

North Dakota
University of North Dakota

Ohio
Ohio State University

Oklahoma
University of Oklahoma

Oregon
University of Oregon

Pennsylvania
Pennsylvania State University
Temple University

Rhode Island
University of Rhode Island

South Carolina
Clemson University
University of South Carolina

South Dakota
University of South Dakota

Tennessee
University of Tennessee

Texas

Texas A&M University
University of Houston
University of Texas

Utah

University of Utah

Vermont

University of Vermont

Virginia

College of William & Mary
Virginia Polytechnic Institute (Virginia Tech)
University of Virginia

Washington

University of Washington

West Virginia

West Virginia University

Wisconsin

University of Wisconsin-Madison

Wyoming

University of Wyoming

Non-Flagship State Schools

Alabama

Alabama A&M University
Alabama State University
Athens State University

Auburn University at Montgomery
Jacksonville State University
Troy University
Troy University Dothan
Troy University Montgomery
Troy University Phoenix City
University of Alabama at Birmingham
University of Alabama in Huntsville
University of Montevallo
University of North Alabama
University of South Alabama
University of West Alabama

Alaska
University of Alaska Anchorage
University of Alaska Fairbanks
University of Alaska Southeast

Arizona
Northern Arizona University

Arkansas
Arkansas State University
Arkansas Tech University
Henderson State University
Southern Arkansas University
University of Arkansas at Fort Smith
University of Arkansas at Little Rock
University of Arkansas at Monticello
University of Arkansas at Pine Bluff
University of Central Arkansas

California
California Maritime Academy
California Polytechnic State University San Luis Obispo

California State Polytechnic University Pomona
California State University Bakersfield
California State University Channel Island
California State University Chico
California State University Dominguez Hills
California State University East Bay
California State University Fresno
California State University Fullerton
California State University Long Beach
California State University Los Angeles
California State University Monterey Bay
California State University Northridge
California State University Sacramento
California State University San Bernardino
California State University San Marcos
California State University Stanislaus
Humboldt State University
San Diego State University
San Francisco State University
San Jose State University
Sonoma State University
University of California Davis
University of California Irvine
University of California Los Angeles (UCLA)
University of California Merced
University of California Riverside
University of California San Diego
University of California San Francisco
University of California Santa Barbara
University of California Santa Cruz

Colorado

Adams State College
Colorado Mesa University
Colorado School of Mines

Colorado State University
Colorado State University-Pueblo
Fort Lewis College
Metropolitan State College of Denver
University of Colorado Colorado Springs
University of Colorado Denver
University of Northern Colorado
Western State College of Colorado

Connecticut

Central Connecticut State University
Eastern Connecticut State University
Southern Connecticut State University
Western Connecticut State University

Delaware

Delaware State University

Florida

Chipola College
Daytona State College
Edison State College
Florida A&M University
Florida Atlantic University
Florida Gulf Coast University
Florida International University
Florida State College at Jacksonville
Florida State University
Indian River State College
Miami Dade College
New College of Florida
Northwest Florida State College
Palm Beach State College
St. Petersburg College

Santa Fe College
University of Central Florida
University of North Florida
University of South Florida
University of West Florida

Georgia

Albany State University
Armstrong-Atlantic State University
Augusta State University
Clayton State University
Columbus State University
Dalton State University
Fort Valley State University
Georgia College and State University
Georgia Gwinnett College
Georgia Institute of Technology
Georgia Southern University
Georgia Southwestern State University
Georgia State University
Kennesaw State University
Macon State College
Medical College of Georgia
Middle Georgia College
North Georgia College and State University
Savannah State University
Southern Polytechnic State University
University of North Georgia
University of West Georgia
Valdosta State University

Hawaii

University of Hawaii at Hilo
University of Hawaii-West Oahu

Idaho

Boise State University
Idaho State University
Lewis-Clark State College

Illinois

Chicago State University
Eastern Illinois University
Governors State University
Illinois State University
· Northeastern Illinois University
Northern Illinois University
Southern Illinois University Carbondale
Southern Illinois University Edwardsville
University of Illinois at Chicago
University of Illinois at Springfield
Western Illinois University

Indiana

Ball State University
Indiana State University
Indiana University East
Indiana University Kokomo
Indiana University Northwest
Indiana University South Bend
Indiana University Southeast
Indiana University-Purdue University Fort Wayne
Indiana University-Purdue U. Indianapolis
Purdue University Calumet
Purdue University North Central
University of Southern Indiana
Vincennes University

Iowa

Iowa State University
University of Northern Iowa

Kansas

Emporia State University
Fort Hays State University
Kansas State University
Pittsburg State University
Washburn University
Wichita State University

Kentucky

Eastern Kentucky University
Kentucky State University
Morehead State University
Murray State University
Northern Kentucky University
Western Kentucky University

Louisiana

Grambling State University
Louisiana State University Alexandria
Louisiana State University Shreveport
Louisiana Tech University
McNeese State University
Nicholls State University
Northwestern State University
Southeastern Louisiana University
Southern University at Baton Rouge
Southern University at New Orleans
University of Louisiana at Lafayette
University of Louisiana at Monroe
University of New Orleans

Maine

Maine Maritime Academy
University of Maine at Augusta
University of Maine at Farmington
University of Maine at Fort Kent

University of Maine at Machias
University of Maine at Presque Isle
University of Southern Maine

Maryland

Bowie State University
Coppin State University
Frostburg State University
Morgan State University
St. Mary's College of Maryland
Salisbury State University
Towson University
University of Baltimore
University of Maryland, Baltimore
University of Maryland, Baltimore County
University of Maryland, Eastern Shore
University of Maryland, University College

Massachusetts

Bridgewater State University
Fitchburg State University
Framingham State University
Massachusetts College of Art and Design
Massachusetts College of Liberal Arts
Massachusetts Maritime Academy
Salem State University
University of Massachusetts Boston
University of Massachusetts Dartmouth
University of Massachusetts Lowell
Westfield State University
Worcester State University

Michigan

Central Michigan University
Eastern Michigan University

Ferris State University
Grand Valley State University
Lake Superior State University
Michigan Technological University
Northern Michigan University
Oakland University
Saginaw Valley State University
University of Michigan-Flint
University of Michigan-Dearborn
Wayne State University
Western Michigan University

Minnesota

Bemidji State University
Metropolitan State University
Minnesota State University Mankato
Minnesota State University Moorhead
Southwest Minnesota State University
St. Cloud State University
University of Minnesota, Crookston
University of Minnesota, Duluth
University of Minnesota, Morris
University of Minnesota, Rochester
Winona State University

Mississippi

Alcorn State University
Delta State University
Jackson State University
Mississippi State University
Mississippi University for Women
Mississippi Valley State University
University of Mississippi Medical Center
University of Southern Mississippi

Missouri

Harris-Stowe State University
Lincoln University of Missouri
Missouri Southern State University
Missouri State University
Missouri University of Science and Technology
Missouri Western State University
Northwest Missouri State University
Southeast Missouri State University
Truman State University
University of Central Missouri
University of Missouri-Kansas City
University of Missouri-St Louis

Montana

Montana State University-Billings
Montana State University-Bozeman
Montana State University-Northern
Montana Tech of the University of Montana
Salish Kootenai College
University of Montana Western

Nebraska

Chadron State College
Peru State College
University of Nebraska at Kearney
University of Nebraska at Omaha
University of Nebraska Medical Center
Wayne State College

Nevada

College of Southern Nevada
Great Basin College
Nevada State College
University of Nevada, Reno

New Hampshire
Granite State University
Keene State College
Plymouth State University

New Jersey
College of New Jersey
Kean University
Montclair State University
New Jersey City University
New Jersey Institute of Technology
Ramapo College of New Jersey
Richard Stockton College of New Jersey
Rowan University
Rutgers University–Newark
Rutgers University–Camden
Thomas Edison State College
William Paterson University

New Mexico
Eastern New Mexico University
Institute of American Indian Arts
New Mexico Highlands University
New Mexico Institute of Mining and Technology
New Mexico State University
Northern New Mexico College
Western New Mexico University

New York
Binghamton University/SUNY
Buffalo State College/SUNY
City University of New York
Fashion Institute of Technology
Morrisville State College
State University of NY Alfred State College

State University of NY at Brockport
State University of NY at Canton
State University of NY at Cobleskill
State University of NY at Cortland
State University of NY at Delhi
State University of NY Empire State College
State University of NY at Farmingdale
State University of NY at Fredonia
State University of NY at Geneseo
State University of NY Health Science Center
State University of NY Institute of Technology
State University of NY Maritime College
State University of NY at New Paltz
State University of NY at Old Westbury
State University of NY at Oneonta
State University of NY at Oswego
State University of NY at Plattsburgh
State University of NY at Potsdam
State University of NY at Purchase
State University of NY Upstate Medical University
Stony Brook University/SUNY
University at Albany/SUNY
University at Buffalo/SUNY

North Carolina

Appalachian State University
East Carolina University
Elizabeth City State University
Fayetteville State University
North Carolina A&T State University
North Carolina Central University
University of North Carolina at Asheville
University of North Carolina at Charlotte
University of North Carolina at Greensboro
University of North Carolina at Pembroke

University of North Carolina at Wilmington
University of North Carolina School of the Arts
Western Carolina University
Winston-Salem State University

North Dakota
Bismarck State College
Dickinson State University
Mayville State University
Minot State University
North Dakota State College of Science
North Dakota State University
Valley City State University

Ohio
Bowling Green State University
Bowling Green State University-Firelands
Central State University
Cleveland State University
Kent State University Kent (main campus)
Kent State University Ashtabula
Kent State University East Liverpool
Kent State University Geauga
Kent State University Salem
Kent State University Stark
Kent State University Trumbull
Kent State University Tuscarawas
Miami University
Miami University Hamilton
Miami University Middletown
Ohio State University Lima
Ohio State University Mansfield
Ohio State University Marion
Ohio State University Newark
Ohio University Athens

Ohio University Chillicothe
Ohio University Eastern
Ohio University Lancaster
Ohio University Southern
Ohio University Zanesville
Shawnee State University
University of Akron
University of Cincinnati
University of Toledo
Wright State University
Youngstown State University

Oklahoma

Cameron University
East Central University
Langston University
Northeastern State University
Northwestern Oklahoma State University
Oklahoma Panhandle State University
Oklahoma State University
Oklahoma State University-Oklahoma City
Oklahoma State University-Tulsa
Oklahoma State University Institute of Technology
Rogers State University
Southeastern Oklahoma State University
Southwestern Oklahoma State University
University of Central Oklahoma
University of Oklahoma Health Sciences Center
University of Science and Arts of Oklahoma

Oregon

Eastern Oregon University
Oregon Institute of Technology
Oregon State Institute of Technology
Oregon State University

Portland State University
Southern Oregon University
Western Oregon University

Pennsylvania

Bloomsburg University of Pennsylvania
California University of Pennsylvania
Cheyney University of Pennsylvania
Clarion University of Pennsylvania
East Stroudsburg University of Pennsylvania
Edinboro University of Pennsylvania
Indiana University of Pennsylvania
Kutztown University of Pennsylvania
Lincoln University
Lock Haven University of Pennsylvania
Mansfield University of Pennsylvania
Millersville University of Pennsylvania
Pennsylvania State University Abington
Pennsylvania State University Altoona
Pennsylvania State University Beaver
Pennsylvania State University Berks
Pennsylvania State University Brandywine
Pennsylvania State University DuBois
Pennsylvania State University Erie
Pennsylvania State University Fayette
Pennsylvania State University Greater Allegheny
Pennsylvania State University Harrisburg
Pennsylvania State University Hazleton
Pennsylvania State University Lehigh Valley
Pennsylvania State University Mount Alto
Pennsylvania State University New Kensington
Pennsylvania State University Schuylkill
Pennsylvania State University Shenango
Pennsylvania State University Wilkes-Barre
Pennsylvania State University Worthington Scranton

Pennsylvania State University York
Pennsylvania College of Technology
Shippensburg University of Pennsylvania
Slippery Rock University of Pennsylvania
University of Pittsburgh
University of Pittsburgh at Bradford
University of Pittsburgh at Greensburg
University of Pittsburgh at Johnstown
University of Pittsburgh at Titusville
West Chester University of Pennsylvania

Puerto Rico
Puerto Rico Conservatory of Music

Rhode Island
Rhode Island College

South Carolina
The Citadel
Coastal Carolina University
College of Charleston
Francis Marion University
Lander University
Medical University of South Carolina
South Carolina State University
University of South Carolina Aiken
University of South Carolina Beaufort
University of South Carolina Lancaster
University of South Carolina Salkehatchie
University of South Carolina Sumter
University of South Carolina Union
University of South Carolina Upstate
Winthrop University

South Dakota
Black Hills State University
Dakota State University
Northern State University
Oglala Lakota College
Sinte Gleska College
South Dakota School of Mines & Technology
South Dakota State University

Tennessee
Austin Peay State University
East Tennessee State University
Middle Tennessee State University
Tennessee State University
Tennessee Technological University
University of Memphis
University of Memphis Lambuth
University of Tennessee Knoxville
University of Tennessee Martin

Texas
Angelo State University
Lamar University
Midwestern State University
Prairie View A&M University
Sam Houston State University
Stephen F. Austin State University
Sul Ross State University
Tarleton State University
Texas A&M University-Central Texas
Texas A&M University-Commerce
Texas A&M University-Corpus Christi
Texas A&M University-Kingsville
Texas A&M University-San Antonio
Texas A&M University-Texarkana

Texas A&M International University
Texas Southern University
Texas State University San Marcos
Texas Tech University
Texas Tech University HSC School of Nursing
Texas Women's University
University of Houston-Clear Lake
University of Houston-Downtown
University of Houston-Victoria
University of North Texas
University of Texas Arlington
University of Texas Brownsville
University of Texas Dallas
University of Texas El Paso
University of Texas Health Science Center
University of Texas Medical Branch
University of Texas Pan American
University of Texas San Antonio
University of Texas Southwestern Medical Center
University of Texas of the Permian Basin
University of Texas Tyler
West Texas A&M University

Utah

College of Eastern Utah
Dixie State College of Utah
Southern Utah University
Utah State University
Utah Valley University
Weber State University

Vermont

Castleton State College
Johnson State College
Lyndon State College
Vermont Technical College

Virgin Islands

University of the Virgin Islands

Virginia

Christopher Newport University
George Mason University
James Madison University
Longwood University
Norfolk State University
Old Dominion University
Radford University
University of Mary Washington
University of Virginia College at Wise
Virginia Commonwealth University
Virginia Military Institute
Virginia State University

Washington

Bellevue College
Central Washington University
Eastern Washington University
Evergreen State College
Olympic College
University of Washington Bothell
University of Washington Tacoma
Washington State University
Washington State University Spokane
Washington State University Tri-Cities
Washington State University Vancouver
Western Washington University

West Virginia

Bluefield State College
Concord University
Fairmont State University
Glenville State College

Marshall University
Mountain State University
Shepherd University
West Liberty University
West Virginia State University
West Virginia University Institute of Technology
West Virginia University at Parkersburg

Wisconsin

University of Wisconsin-Eau Claire
University of Wisconsin-Green Bay
University of Wisconsin–La Crosse
University of Wisconsin-Milwaukee
University of Wisconsin-Parkside
University of Wisconsin-Oshkosh
University of Wisconsin-Platteville
University of Wisconsin-River Falls
University of Wisconsin-Stevens Point
University of Wisconsin-Stout
University of Wisconsin-Superior
University of Wisconsin-Whitewater

Highly Selective Private Colleges

California

California Institute of Technology
Claremont McKenna College
Harvey Mudd College
Occidental College
Pepperdine University
Pomona College
Scripps College
Stanford University
University of Southern California

Colorado
Colorado College

Connecticut
Connecticut College
Trinity College
Wesleyan University
Yale University

District of Columbia
George Washington University
Georgetown University

Florida
University of Miami

Georgia
Emory University

Illinois
Northwestern University
University of Chicago

Indiana
University of Notre Dame

Iowa
Grinnell College

Kentucky
Centre College

Louisiana
Tulane University

Maine

Bates College
Bowdoin College
Clark University
Colby College

Maryland

Johns Hopkins University

Massachusetts

Amherst College
Boston College
Boston University
College of the Holy Cross
Franklin W. Olin College of Engineering
Harvard University
Massachusetts Institute of Technology
Mount Holyoke College
Smith College
Tufts University
Wellesley College
Williams College

Minnesota

Carleton College
Macalester College

Missouri

Washington University

New Hampshire

Dartmouth College

New Jersey

Princeton University
Stevens Institute of Technology

New York
Bard College
Barnard College–Columbia University
Clarkson University
Colgate University
Columbia University
Cooper Union
Cornell University
Fordham University
Hamilton College
Manhattan School of Music
New York University
Polytechnic Institute of New York
Rensselaer Polytechnic Institute
Union College
University of Rochester
Vassar College
Webb Institute

North Carolina
Davidson College
Duke University
Wake Forest University

Ohio
Case Western Reserve University
Denison University
Kenyon College
Oberlin College
Wilberforce University

Oklahoma
University of Tulsa

Oregon
Reed College

Pennsylvania
Bryn Mawr College
Bucknell University
Dickinson College
Haverford College
Lafayette College
Lehigh University
Swarthmore College
University of Pennsylvania
Villanova University

Rhode Island
Brown University

Tennessee
Rhodes College
Vanderbilt University

Texas
Rice University

Utah
Brigham Young University

Vermont
Middlebury College

Virginia
University of Richmond
Washington and Lee University

Washington
Whitman College

Midsize Private Colleges

California
Loyola Marymount University
Santa Clara University

Colorado
University of Denver

Connecticut
Quinnipiac University

District of Columbia
American University
Catholic University of America
Howard University

Florida
University of Tampa

Idaho
Brigham Young University–Idaho

Illinois
Bradley University
Columbia College
Concordia University Chicago
DePaul University
Lewis University
Loyola University

Indiana
Butler University

Massachusetts
Northeastern University
Suffolk University

Minnesota
University of St. Thomas

Missouri
Lindenwood University
Saint Louis University

Nebraska
Creighton University

New Jersey
Fairleigh Dickinson University

New York
Hofstra University
Ithaca College
Long Island University
New York Institute of Technology
Rochester Institute of Technology
St. John's University
Syracuse University

Ohio
Franklin University
University of Dayton

Pennsylvania
Carnegie Mellon University
Drexel University
Duquesne University

Texas
Baylor University

Utah
Brigham Young University
Southern Methodist University
Texas Christian University

Virginia
Liberty University

Wisconsin
Marquette University

Traditional Private Colleges

Alabama
Amridge University
Birmingham-Southern College
Concordia College Alabama
Faulkner University
Judson College
Miles College
Oakwood University
Samford University
Southeastern Bible College
Spring Hill College
Stillman College
Talladega College
Tuskegee University
University of Mobile

Alaska
Alaska Pacific University

Arizona

Embry-Riddle Aeronautical University
Prescott College

Arkansas

Ecclesia College
Harding University
Hendrix College
Lyon College
Ouachita Baptist University
University of the Ozarks

California

American International College
Antioch University Los Angeles
Antioch University Santa Barbara
Art Center College of Design
California Baptist University
California College of the Arts
California Institute of the Arts
California Lutheran University
Chapman University
Cogswell Polytechnical College
Columbia College Hollywood
Concordia University
Dominican University of California
Golden Gate University
Holy Names University
Hope International University
Humphreys College
John F. Kennedy University
La Sierra University
Life Pacific College
Lincoln University
Marymount College

Menlo College
Mills College
Mount St. Mary's College
Notre Dame de Mamur University
Otis College of Art & Design
Pacific Oaks College
Pacific Union College
Patten University
Pitzer College
Point Loma Nazarene University
Saint Mary's College of California
Samuel Merritt University
Thomas Aquinas College
University of La Verne
University of Redlands
University of San Diego
University of San Francisco
University of the Pacific
Vanguard University
Westmont College
Whittier College
Woodbury University

Colorado

Colorado Christian University
Johnson & Wales University Denver
Regis University
Rocky Mountain College of Art and Design

Connecticut

Albertus Magnus College
Fairfield University
Holy Apostles College
Lyme Academy College of Fine Arts
Mitchell College

Post University
Sacred Heart University
Saint Joseph College
Trinity College
University of Bridgeport
University of Hartford
University of New Haven
University of Saint Joseph

Delaware
Goldey Beacom College
Wesley College
Wilmington University

District of Columbia
Gallaudet University
Southeastern University
Trinity Washington University

Florida
Ave Maria University
Baptist College of Florida
Barry University
Beacon College
Bethune-Cookman University
Eckerd College
Edward Waters College
Embry-Riddle Aeronautical University
Flagler College
Florida Christian College
Florida College
Florida Institute of Technology
Florida Memorial University
Florida Southern College
Hodges University

Jacksonville University
Johnson & Wales University North Miami
Jones College
Lynn University
Northwood University, Florida
Nova Southeastern University
Palm Beach Atlantic University
Pensacola Christian College
Ringling College of Art and Design
Rollins College
Saint John Vianney College Seminary
Saint Leo University
Schiller International University
St. Thomas University
Stetson University
Trinity Baptist College
Webber International University

Georgia

Agnes Scott College
Berry College
Brenau University
Brewton-Parker College
Clark Atlanta University
Covenant College
Emmanuel College
LaGrange College
Life University
Luther Rice Seminary & University
Mercer University
Morehouse College
Morris Brown College
Oglethorpe University
Piedmont College
Reinhardt University

Shorter University
Spelman College
Thomas University
Truett-McConnell College
Wesleyan College
Young Harris College

Hawaii
Chaminade University
Hawaii Pacific University

Idaho
College of Idaho
New Saint Andrews College
Northwest Nazarene University

Illinois
Augustana College
Aurora University
Benedictine University
Blackburn College
Concordia University
Dominican University
Elmhurst College
Eureka College
Illinois College
Illinois Institute of Technology
Illinois Wesleyan University
Judson University
Knox College
Lake Forest College
Lexington College
MacMurray College
McKendree University
Methodist College of Nursing

Millikin University
Monmouth College
National Louis University
North Central College
North Park University
Olivet Nazarene University
Quincy University
Robert Morris University
Rockford College
Roosevelt University
Saint Xavier University
School of the Art Institute of Chicago
Shimer College
Trinity Christian College
Trinity International University
University of St. Francis
Wheaton College

Indiana

Anderson University
Bethel College
Calumet College of St. Joseph
DePauw University
Earlham College
Fairhaven Baptist College
Franklin College
Hanover College
Holy Cross College
Indiana Institute of Technology
Manchester University
Marian University
Rose-Hulman Institute of Technology
St. Joseph's College
St. Mary's College
Saint Mary's College

Saint Mary-of-the-Woods College
Taylor University
Trine University
University of Evansville
University of Indianapolis
University of Saint Francis
Valparaiso University
Wabash College

Iowa

Allen College
Briar Cliff University
Buena Vista University
Central College
Clarke University
Coe College
Cornell College
Divine Word College
Dordt College
Drake University
Grand View University
Loras College
Luther College
Morningside College
Northwestern College
Palmer College of Chiropractic
Simpson College
St. Ambrose University
St. Luke's College
University of Dubuque
Upper Iowa University
Wartburg College
William Penn University

Kansas

Baker University
Barclay College
Benedictine College
Bethany College
Bethel College
Central Christian College
Donnelly College
Friends University
Kansas Wesleyan University
Mid-America Nazarene University
Newman University
Ottawa University
Southwestern College
Sterling College
University of Saint Mary

Kentucky

Asbury University
Bellarmine University
Berea College
Boyce College
Brescia University
Campbellsville University
Georgetown College
Kentucky Christian University
Kentucky Wesleyan College
Lindsey Wilson College
Mid-Continent University
Midway College
St. Catharine College
Simmons College of Kentucky
Spalding University
Thomas More College
Transylvania University

Union College
University of the Cumberlands
University of Pikesville

Louisiana

Centenary College of Louisiana
Dillard University
Louisiana College
Loyola University
Our Lady of Holy Cross College
Our Lady of the Lake College
Xavier University of Louisiana

Maine

College of the Atlantic
Husson University
Maine College of Art
Saint Joseph's College of Maine
Thomas College
Unity College
University of New England

Maryland

Capitol College
College of Notre Dame
Goucher College
Hood College
Loyola University
McDaniel College
Mount St. Mary's University
Notre Dame of Maryland University
Peabody Institute of Johns Hopkins University
Sojourner-Douglass College
St. John's College, Maryland
St. Mary's Seminary & University

Stevenson University
Washington Adventist University
Washington Bible College
Washington College

Massachusetts

Anna Maria College
Assumption College
Atlantic Union College
Babson College
Bard College at Simon's Rock
Bay Path College
Becker College
Bentley University
Berklee College of Music
Boston Architectural College
Boston Conservatory
Brandeis University
Curry College
Dean College
Eastern Nazarene College
Elms College
Emerson College
Emmanuel College
Endicott College
Fisher College
Hampshire College
Hebrew College
Hellenic College
Lasell College
Lesley University
Massachusetts College of Pharmacy and Health Sciences
Merrimack College
Mount Ida College
New England Conservatory of Music

Newbury College
Nichols College
Pine Manor College
Regis College
School of the Museum of Fine Arts
Simmons College
Springfield College
Stonehill College
Wentworth Institute of Technology
Western New England College
Wheaton College
Wheelock College
Worcester Polytechnic Institute

Michigan

Adrian College
Albion College
Alma College
Aquinas College
Calvin College
Cleary University
College for Creative Studies
Concordia University
Cornerstone University
Davenport University
Finlandia University
Great Lakes Christian College
Hillsdale College
Kalamazoo College
Kettering University
Kuyper College
Lawrence Technological University
Madonna University
Northwood University
Olivet College

Rochester College
Sacred Heart Major Seminary
Siena Heights University
Spring Arbor University
University of Detroit Mercy

Minnesota

Augsburg College
Bethany Lutheran College
Bethel University
College of Saint Benedict and Saint John's University
College of St. Scholastica
College of Visual Arts
Concordia University
Crossroads College
Gustavus Adolphus College
Hamline University
Martin Luther College
North Central University
Northwestern College
Oak Hills Christian College
Saint Mary's University of Minnesota
St. Catherine University
St. Olaf College
Saint Thomas University

Mississippi

Belhaven University
Blue Mountain College
Millsaps College
Mississippi College
Rust College
Southeastern Baptist College
Tougaloo College
William Carey University

Missouri

Avila University
Baptist Bible College
Central Bible College
Central Christian College of the Bible
Central Methodist University
College of the Ozarks
Columbia College
Conception Seminary College
Cox College
Culver-Stockton College
Drury University
Evangel University
Fontbonne University
Goldfarb School of Nursing at Barnes-Jewish College
Hannibal-LaGrange University
Kansas City Art Institute
Logan College of Chiropractic
Maryville University
Missouri Baptist University
Missouri Valley College
Ozark Christian College
Park University
Research College of Nursing
Rockhurst University
Saint Luke's College of Health Sciences
Southwest Baptist University
Stephens College
Webster University
Westminster College
William Jewell College
William Woods University

Montana

Carroll College

Rocky Mountain College
University of Great Falls

Nebraska
Bellevue University
Bryan LGH College of Health Sciences
Clarkson College
College of Saint Mary
Concordia University
Doane College
Hastings College
Midland University
Nebraska Christian College
Nebraska Methodist College of Nursing
Nebraska Wesleyan University
St. Gregory the Great Seminary
Summit Christian College
Union College
York College

Nevada
Sierra Nevada College

New Hampshire
Colby-Sawyer College
College of Saint Mary Magdalen
New England College
Rivier College
Saint Anselm College
Southern New Hampshire University
Thomas More College of Liberal Arts

New Jersey
Bloomfield College
Caldwell College

Centenary College
College of Saint Elizabeth
Felician College
Georgian Court University
Monmouth University
Rabbinical College of America
Rider University
Saint Peter's College
Seton Hall University

New Mexico

St. John's College, New Mexico
University of the Southwest

New York

Adelphi University
Albany College of Pharmacy and Health Sciences
Alfred University
Boricua College
Briarcliffe College
Canisius College
Cazenovia College
College of Mount Saint Vincent
College of New Rochelle
College of Saint Rose
Concordia College New York
Culinary Institute of America
D'Youville College
Daemen College
Davis College
Dominican College
Dowling College
Eastman School of Music
Elmira College
Eugene Lang College, New School for Liberal Arts

Hartwick College
Hilbert College
Hobart and William Smith Colleges
Iona College
Jewish Theological Seminary
Juilliard School
Keuka College
Le Moyne College
LIM College
Manhattan College
Manhattanville College
Mannes College, New School of Music
Marist College
Marymount Manhattan College
Medaille College
Mercy College
Metropolitan College of New York
Molloy College
Mount Saint Mary College
Nazareth College of Rochester
New York School of Interior Design
Niagara University
Pace University
Paul Smith's College
Pratt Institute
Roberts Wesleyan College
Russell Sage College
Sage College of Albany
Sarah Lawrence College
Siena College
Skidmore College
St. Bonaventure University
St. Francis College
St. John Fisher College
Saint Joseph's University

St. Lawrence University
St. Thomas Aquinas College
Utica College
Vaughn College of Aeronautics and Technology
Villa Maria College
Wagner College
Wells College
Yeshiva University

North Carolina

Barber-Scotia College
Barton College
Belmont Abbey College
Bennett College
Brevard College
Cabarrus College of Health Sciences
Campbell University
Carolina Christian College
Catawba College
Chowan University
Elon University
Gardner-Webb University
Greensboro College
Guilford College
High Point University
Johnson & Wales University Charlotte
Johnson C. Smith University
Lees-McRae College
Lenoir-Rhyne University
Mars Hill College
Meredith College
Methodist University
Mid-Atlantic Christian University
North Carolina Wesleyan College
Peace College

Pfeiffer University
Piedmont Baptist College
Queens University of Charlotte
Shaw University
St. Andrews University
Saint Augustine's College
Warren Wilson College
Wingate University

North Dakota

Jamestown College
Medcenter One College of Nursing
Trinity Bible College
University of Mary

Ohio

Antioch University McGregor
Art Academy of Cincinnati
Baldwin Wallace University
Capital University
Cedarville University
Cincinnati Christian University
Cleveland Institute of Art
College of Mount St. Joseph
College of Wooster
Columbus College of Art and Design
Defiance College
Franciscan University of Steubenville
God's Bible School and College
Heidelberg University
Hiram College
John Carroll University
Kettering College
Lake Erie College
Lourdes College

Malone University
Marietta College
Mercy College of Ohio
Mount Carmel College of Nursing
Mount Vernon Nazarene University
Muskingum University
Notre Dame College of Ohio
Ohio Christian University
Ohio Dominican University
Ohio Mid-Western College
Ohio Northern University
Ohio Valley University
Ohio Wesleyan University
Otterbein College
Pontifical College Josephinum
Tiffin University
Union Institute and University
University of Findlay
University of Mountain Union
University of Northwestern Ohio
University of Rio Grande
Urbana University
Ursuline College
Walsh University
Wilmington College
Wittenberg University
Xavier University

Oklahoma

Mid-America Christian University
Oklahoma Baptist University
Oklahoma Christian University
Oklahoma City University
Oral Roberts University
St. Gregory's University
Southern Nazarene University

Oregon

Concordia University
Corban University
George Fox University
Lewis & Clark College
Linfield College
Marylhurst University
Mount Angel Seminary
Northwest Christian University
Pacific Northwest College of Art
Pacific University
University of Portland
Warner Pacific College
Willamette University

Pennsylvania

Albright College
Allegheny College
Arcadia University
Baptist Bible College of Pennsylvania
Cabrini College
Cedar Crest College
Central Pennsylvania College
Chatham University
Chestnut Hill College
Delaware Valley College
DeSales University
Elizabethtown College
Franklin & Marshall College
Gannon University
Geneva College
Gettysburg College
Gratz College
Grove City College
Gwynedd-Mercy College
Holy Family University

Immaculata University
Juniata College
Keystone College
King's College
Lancaster Bible College
La Roche College
La Salle University
Lebanon Valley College
Lycoming College
Marywood University
Mercyhurst University
Misericordia University
Moore College of Art and Design
Mount Aloysius College
Muhlenberg College
Neumann University
Peirce College
Pennsylvania College of Art and Design
Philadelphia University
Point Park University
Robert Morris University
Rosemont College
Saint Francis University
Saint Vincent College
Seton Hill University
Susquehanna University
The Restaurant School at Walnut Hill College
Thiel College
Thomas Jefferson University
University of Scranton
University of the Arts
University of the Sciences in Philadelphia
Ursinus College
Valley Forge Christian College
Washington & Jefferson College

Waynesburg University
Westminster College
Widener University
Wilkes University
Wilson College
York College of Pennsylvania

Rhode Island

Bryant University
Johnson & Wales University Providence
New England Institute of Technology
Providence College
Rhode Island School of Design
Roger Williams University
Salve Regina University

South Carolina

Allen University
Anderson University
Benedict College
Bob Jones University
Charleston Southern University
Claflin University
Coker College
Converse College
Erskine College
Furman University
Morris College
Newberry College
North Greenville University
Presbyterian College
Southern Wesleyan University
Voorhees College
Wofford College

South Dakota

Augustana College
Dakota Wesleyan University
Mount Marty College
Presentation College
University of Sioux Falls

Tennessee

American Baptist College
Aquinas College
Baptist Memorial College Health Sciences
Belmont University
Bethel University
Bryan College
Carson–Newman College
Christian Brothers University
Cumberland University
Fisk University
Freed–Hardeman University
Johnson University
King College
Knoxville College
Lee University
LeMoyne–Owen College
Lincoln Memorial University
Lipscomb University
Martin Methodist College
Maryville College
Memphis College of Art
O'More College of Design
Southern Adventist University
Tennessee Temple University
Tennessee Wesleyan College
Trevecca Nazarene University
Tusculum College

Union University
University of the South
Visible Music College

Texas

Abilene Christian University
Amberton University
Arlington Baptist College
Austin College
College of Saint Thomas More
Concordia University
Criswell College
Dallas Baptist University
Dallas Christian College
East Texas Baptist University
Hardin-Simmons University
Houston Baptist University
Huston-Tillotson University
Jarvis Christian College
Lone Star Baptist College
Lubbock Christian University
McMurry University
Northwood University
Our Lady of the Lake University
Paul Quinn College
Schreiner University
Southwestern Adventist University
Southwestern Assemblies of God University
Southwestern University
St. Edward's University
St. Mary's University
Texas Chiropractic College
Texas Lutheran University
Texas Wesleyan University
Trinity University

University of Dallas
University of the Incarnate Word
University of Mary Hardin-Baylor
University of St. Thomas
Wayland Baptist University
Wiley College

Utah

Westminster College

Vermont

Bennington College
Burlington College
Champlain College
College of St. Joseph
Goddard College
Green Mountain College
Marlboro College
Norwich University
Saint Michael's College
Southern Vermont College
Sterling College

Virginia

Bluefield College
Bridgewater College
Christendom College
Eastern Mennonite University
Emory & Henry College
Ferrum College
Hampden-Sydney College
Hampton University
Hollins University
Jefferson College of Health Sciences
Lynchburg College

Mary Baldwin College
Marymount University
Randolph-Macon College
Roanoke College
Shenandoah University
Southern Virginia University
Sweet Briar College
Virginia Intermont College
Virginia Union University
Virginia University of Lynchburg
Virginia Wesleyan College

Washington

City University of Seattle
Gonzaga University
Heritage University
Northwest University
Pacific Lutheran University
Saint Martin's University
Seattle Pacific University
Trinity Lutheran College
University of Puget Sound
Walla Walla University
Whitworth University

West Virginia

Alderson-Broaddus College
Appalachian Bible College
Bethany College
Davis and Elkins College
Salem International University
St. Mary's Medical Center School of Nursing
University of Charleston
West Virginia Wesleyan College
Wheeling Jesuit University

Wisconsin

Alverno College
Bellin College
Beloit College
Carroll University
Carthage College
Columbia College of Nursing
Concordia University
Edgewood College
Immanuel Lutheran College
Lawrence University
Marian University
Milwaukee Institute of Art and Design
Milwaukee School of Engineering
Mount Mary College
Northland College
Ripon College
St. Norbert College
Silver Lake College
Viterbo University
Wisconsin Lutheran College

Wyoming

Wyoming Catholic College

GLOSSARY

Academic fit—Achieved if the college has the major or program the student wants to pursue, and his or her GPA and standardized test scores match up with those of the school's median population.

Affordability—The amount that a family can afford to spend on college each year.

Affordability threshold—The maximum amount of money that a family has available to spend on college each year.

AGI (adjusted gross income)—The bottom line of the front page of a IRS 1040 tax form.

Appeal—Family's request to the college's financial aid office to consider additional circumstances, such as a change in the family's financial situation or added expenses, since the FAFSA was filed. Reasons to appeal might include loss of income, medical or health-related expenses, educational costs of the student's younger siblings, or extraordinary circumstances.

Application fee—Fee charged by colleges as part of the admission process and sent in with the application.

Assets—Defined for FAFSA purposes as savings and investments. For parents, that includes cash, savings, checking accounts, money market accounts, mutual funds, and individual stocks and bonds, but not the equity of the parents' home or the value of retirement plans such as annuities and IRAs.

Asset protection allowance—Every family receives an asset protection allowance on the FAFSA. Based on the oldest parent's age and the number of people in the family, the allowance protects some reportable assets.

Award letter—The official document that a college sends to a family after all financial aid forms have been submitted, usually in March or April of the child's senior year. The award letter identifies a family's net price and lists all financial aid programs—including grants, scholarships, loans, and campus employment options—for which the student is eligible.

Capitalizing the interest—Refers to the practice of adding the interest to the principal of an unsubsidized loan and then paying it all off after graduation. Capitalizing the interest can increase the loan balance by 15 to 20 percent by the time the student starts to repay it. A better plan may be for the student to pay the interest ($25 per month, based on the current 6.8 percent interest rate) while in school.

College grant—Money awarded to a student to help pay tuition or other college costs. The grant may come from the federal government, a state agency, or the college itself. Unlike loans, grants do not need to be repaid.

College inflation—Term referring to the fact that college costs are rising at a much more rapid rate than the inflation of the U.S. economy as a whole, make college much less affordable for everyone.

College loan—Direct loan from the college to the student to help pay his or her education costs. These loans are rare and vary in interest rates and repayment terms.

College search programs—These online programs give students access to information on more than 2,000 four-year colleges and universities in the United States and allow them to enter preferences (school location and size, major, extracurricular activities, and more) to create a narrowed-down list of colleges that match the student's interests.

Community college—Local, two-year public college that offers a wide variety of vocational training programs as well as the option of completing general requirements and then transferring to a four-year college. Offers the advantage of greatly reduced tuition costs for district residents. Open admission allows students to improve their GPAs before moving to a four-year school.

Commuting—Living at home and attending a local college, an option that dramatically reduces net price by eliminating the cost of room and board.

Cost of attendance—Term used by colleges to identify their comprehensive college cost, which includes tuition and fees, room and board, transportation, books and supplies, and personal expenses. Also referred to as **sticker price**.

CSS Profile—A supplemental financial aid form that some colleges require families to complete in addition to the FAFSA. Provides more detailed financial information than the FAFSA and is required by some Ivy League and other highly selective private schools. College financial aid officers use results of the profile to frame the financial aid letters they send to students.

Glossary

Custodial account—A Section 529 prepaid tuition program or other account that lists the child as the owner and the parent or other adult as the custodian.

Direct costs of attendance—Tuition and fees, and room-and-board costs of attending a college. Direct costs are not the same as the **cost of attendance**, which also includes books, transportation, and personal expenses.

Direct Loan—Loan available through a federal program to any student whose family completes the FAFSA. The per-year borrowing limit for the unsubsidized loan is $5,500 for freshman year, $6,500 for sophomore year, and $7,500 each for junior and senior years, for a maximum of $27,000. (For more on the two types of these loans, see Subsidized Direct Loan and Unsubsidized Direct Loan.)

EFC (Expected Family Contribution)—A number calculated after FAFSA submission that determines a student's eligibility for certain need-based financial aid programs. Generally, the lower the number, the greater the student's eligibility for these programs. This number is *not* the net price, the amount that the student's family is expected to pay out of pocket for college.

Execution Phase—The second part of Financial Fit, in which families understand the EFC and financial aid, including the ten loan options, and complete the FAFSA and possibly the CSS Profile. This phase also includes exploring merit and private scholarships, maximizing the student's benefits, interpreting award letters, and finally choosing the right college at the right price.

Extended repayment—Option of longer payment time allowed for Direct Loans. If the student has accumulated more than $30,000 in student-loan debt, he or she can opt to repay it over ten to thirty years. This lowers the monthly payment but results in paying more interest over the course of the loan.

Estimated net price—The estimated amount that attendance at a college will cost per year, determined by using the school's net price calculator on its website.

FAFSA (Free Application for Federal Student Aid)—The financial aid application that the U.S. government uses to officially determine a family's **EFC** number. FAFSA provides access to need-based financial programs and to federal Direct Loans. The FAFSA is filed on or after January 1 of the child's senior year of high school and must be resubmitted every year the student is in college.

FAFSA4caster—A government software program that allows families to calculate an estimated EFC number in advance of filing the FAFSA. This number can be used in many net price calculators to save from having to complete the income and asset questions requested.

Federal work study (or campus employment)—A campus job awarded based on financial need to a student to lower the cost of attendance.

Right College, Right Price

Feel fit—Achieved if the atmosphere of the college feels right to the prospective student who can imagine himself or herself part of the college culture there.

Financial fit—Achieved if the college's net price is one that the family can afford.

Financial Fit college categories—Eight categories into which U.S. colleges can be grouped based on their price and affordability: flagship state schools, non-flagship state schools, out-of-state flagship state schools, out-of-state non-flagship state schools, highly selective private schools, midsize private schools, traditional private schools, and commuting and/or community college options.

Flagship state school (in state)—The premier state college or university in the state where the family lives; these schools make up one of the Financial Fit college categories. Usually these schools have more students and more stringent admission requirements than other state schools. They offer lower in-state tuition but also may offer fewer scholarships or grants.

Flagship state school (out of state)—The premier state college or university in a state other than where the family lives; these schools make up one of the Financial Fit college categories. Usually these schools have more students and more stringent admission requirements than other state schools.

Gift aid—Grants or scholarships that reduce the overall cost of attendance. This is not money that needs to be repaid.

Graduated repayment—Option for repaying a Direct Loan in which payment is low at first and increased every two years. The lowest payments are obtained through the income-based and extended-repayment options.

Highly selective private college—One of the most prestigious colleges or universities in the country, such as Harvard, Yale, or Stanford; these schools make up one of the Financial Fit college categories. Admission is highly competitive, requiring high grades and test scores. Some of these schools offer substantial assistance to families with financial need.

Home equity loan—An additional loan beyond the mortgage on the parents' home that is paid out in a lump sum to help finance college. Advantages are that interest on a home equity loan is tax deductible and the loan can provide a longer repayment period than a student loan.

Income-based repayment—Option for repaying a Direct Loan that bases the amount of monthly payments on the former student's discretionary income. This is defined as **adjusted gross income** minus 10 percent of the poverty line for the family size.

Independent student—One who is a ward of the court, homeless, in the military, or married, or who is financially supporting children of his or her own.

Also a student who is taking graduate classes or more than twenty-four years old. Students are not considered independent of their parents simply because they were not declared on their parents' tax return.

Line of credit against equity—A home equity line of credit (HELOC) established to pay for college. Instead of borrowing a lump sum, the parents write checks on the line of credit to pay the college, when needed, and only pay only interest to the lender while the student is in college. After that, the parents pay down the principal on the line of credit.

Local scholarships—Private scholarships awarded by community businesses, organizations, and clubs and often available only to students in your high school. These scholarships offer the greatest chance for success because the pool of applicants is very small.

Merit scholarship—Money awarded to a student by a college for academics, athletics, or other special talents to lower the cost of attendance. Merit scholarships are not need based and do not need to be repaid.

Midsized private college—A college grouped in the smallest of the Financial Fit college categories. These schools usually have an enrollment of more than 5,000 students and sticker prices that are lower than those of the highly selective schools but higher than those of the private schools. Schools in this category often offer attractive merit-based scholarships and need-based grants.

Military scholarship opportunities—Three types are offered: admission to one of the U.S. service academies such as West Point, which is a difficult, competitive process; a merit-based military scholarship by joining the Reserve Officer Training Corps (ROTC) and serving as an officer in the armed services after college; or enlisting and receiving tuition assistance.

National scholarships—Private scholarships that are available to students throughout the country and publicized widely online. These scholarships can be difficult to get because of the large, competitive pools of applicants.

NAIA (National Association of Intercollegiate Athletics)—National governing body for approximately 350 small college athletics programs in the United States.

NCAA (National Collegiate Athletic Association)—Association that organizes athletic programs of many U.S. colleges and universities. These schools play sports in three divisions (Division I, Division II, and Division III) that differ in the depth of the sports programs offered. Generally the largest schools compete in Division I and smaller schools in the other two divisions. The NCAA allows Division I and II schools to offer athletes scholarships for playing a sport.

NCAA Eligibility Center—Certifies that registered athletes who wish to compete in NCAA Division I or II athletics programs have the required academic credentials from high school and are amateur athletes. This certification is required to receive merit money. High school students can register online with the eligibility center during their junior year of high school.

Need-based grants—Money awarded for a student to attend college based on that student's financial need. Unlike a loan, grant money does not need to be repaid.

Net price—The actual out-of-pocket cost of a college after grants, scholarships, student loans, and campus employment options have been deducted from the **sticker price**.

Net price calculator—A federally mandated software tool provided on every college's website that allows a family to calculate its **estimated net price** at that school. Note that all colleges do not use the same universal net price calculator, which can complicate making comparisons. Calculators that require parents to provide exact financial information and ask questions about the student's academic performance are the most reliable.

Net price comparison chart—Chart that lists estimated net prices for selected colleges in the Financial Fit college categories for comparison and has been prepared by a family to help determine which college categories and individual schools will fit their affordability threshold.

Non-flagship state school (in state)—A state-supported college or university other than the flagship school in the state where the family lives; these schools make up one of the Financial Fit college categories. These schools may have fewer students and lower admission standards than the flagship school but are not necessarily of lesser quality. These schools offer lower tuition for state residents but usually fewer grants or scholarships than traditional private schools.

Non-flagship state school (out of state)—Not the premier state school but another state-supported college in a state other than where the family lives; these schools make up one of the Financial Fit college categories. These schools may have fewer students and lower admission standards than the flagship school but are not necessarily of lesser quality. They usually offer fewer grants or scholarships than traditional private schools.

Parent loan—Type of loan that the parent, not the student, is responsible for repaying. An example is the federal PLUS loan.

Pell Grant—The largest federal grant program in the country. Eligibility for Pell Grants is determined by the family's **EFC** number. If the number is 4,995 or lower, the student is eligible for a full or partial Pell Grant. Eligibility is determined separately for each year of college.

Glossary

Perkins Loan—Subsidized loan of up to $5,500 a year made to a student with financial need by a college, using funds received from the federal government. No interest accrues on the account until after the student graduates, and repayment begins nine months after graduation. Completing the FAFSA is an eligibility requirement. Colleges usually award these loans on a first-come, first-served basis, giving them to students with the greatest financial need.

Planning Phase—The first part of Financial Fit, in which families assess their affordability and discuss that with their student, as well as understanding the Financial Fit college categories and using colleges' online net price calculators to determine affordability. This phase also includes considering the community college and commuting options to lower costs, and narrowing down the list of colleges under consideration.

PLUS Loan (Parent Loan to Undergraduate Students)—A federal loan option available to parents to help pay for college. The parent, not the student, is responsible for repaying this type of loan, which is not based on financial need. Repayment starts immediately, as does the accrual of interest on the loan. The PLUS loan should *not* be included as a type of financial aid when determining net price.

Prepaid tuition plan (Section 529)—Tax-free college saving plan that allows parents to lock in future tuition rates at state-supported colleges at current prices. Named after Section 529 of the Internal Revenue Code.

Private education loan (or alternative student loan)—Loan offered by a bank or other financial institution, not the federal government. These loans are not based on need, and are not subsidized. While technically student loans, private education loans require a good credit history, which generally means a parent co-signer.

Private scholarship—Money awarded to a student to use for college by businesses, agencies, organizations, and clubs. These may be based on a wide variety of criteria, such parents' type of work, ethnic background, location of residence, student interests or skills, selected college major, service activities, or other factors.

Regional scholarships—Private scholarships awarded to students by their county, city, or state. The competitive pool for these awards is larger than for a local scholarship but still smaller than that of the national scholarships.

Reportable asset—Any of the parent assets required to be reported on the FAFSA. These include funds in cash, savings and checking account on the day the FAFSA is prepared, as well as assets in CDs, mutual funds, individual stocks and bonds, commodities, and equity in real estate other than the family home. Based on the oldest parent's age and the number of people in the family, some reportable assets are protected.

Repositioning of assets—Moving parents' savings and investments into categories that do not have to be reported on the FAFSA document, such as pension plans, IRAs, Roth IRAs, or annuities. In most cases, shifting assets does not result in a significantly lower net price.

Resident assistant (RA)—Student employed by the college to help supervise and manage a floor of a dormitory; usually paid a stipend of $8,000 to $10,000, along with free room and board. Sometimes called a resident advisor.

SAR (Student Aid Report)—Summary sent to families that shows the information they provided on the FAFSA. The SAR should be checked for accuracy and changes made as needed. Colleges that the family selected on the FAFSA and state agencies that award need-based aid receive an electronic version of the SAR, called the ISAR, to use in determining the student's financial aid.

Scholarship search programs—Online programs available on specialized websites that a student can use to narrow down the list of national opportunities and link to information and applications for those that seem most appropriate to pursue. These widely used search programs create pools of thousands of applicants for the scholarships, making them highly competitive.

Standard repayment—The most common repayment option for Direct Loans, which is paying them off over ten years.

State grant—Grant that a student receives from an individual state to help pay college costs. Eligibility may be determined by the family's EFC number, which generally has to be quite low to qualify. The student may have to attend a public or private college in the state.

Sticker price—The advertised price of a college. The sticker price includes tuition and fees, room and board, transportation, books and supplies, and personal expenses. Also referred to as **cost of attendance**. The sticker price is a somewhat meaningless measure without knowing how much the student will receive in grants, scholarships, and student loans.

Student loan—A loan written in the student's name and which the student, not the parents, is legally responsible to pay back with interest. Federal Direct Loans are an example.

Subsidized Direct Loan—Federal student loan offered to students who file the FAFSA and demonstrate financial need. No interest is accrued on subsidized loans until six months after the student graduates from college, and interest rates are lower than those for unsubsidized Direct Loans. Formerly called the Stafford Loan.

Traditional Private school—A school that is not a state school or highly selective private school and generally has fewer than 5,000 students. Some of the schools have maintained a religious identity, while others have not. These schools make up the largest Financial Fit college category of U.S. colleges and universities. They may offer substantial merit awards.

Unsubsidized Direct Loan—Federal student loan for which all students who file the FAFSA are eligible, regardless of need. Interest on unsubsidized loans begins to accrue immediately, and interest rates are higher than those for subsidized Direct Loans. Formerly called the Stafford Loan.

Workplace scholarships—Private scholarships awarded by companies to the children of employees.

INDEX

Index

ACKNOWLEDGMENTS

So many to thank!

To Peter, Tracey, and Lindsay at Sourcebooks for their direction and editing support.

To my family for their patience.

To my colleagues at Hinsdale South for their consistent encouragement.

To the many families with whom I've worked whose struggles in paying for college inspired this book.

And to the many high school counselors and college admissions professionals who understand that the way we have done it for years has had to change. Your openness to teaching Financial Fit is the key to us ending the college debt crisis.

ABOUT THE AUTHOR

Frank Palmasani delivered his first seminar about college financial aid in 1981. At the time he had completed five years of college counseling work on the high school level and was in his first year as an admissions counselor at Lewis University. From 1981 to 1993, Palmasani expanded his role in admissions from counselor to assistant director to associate director and eventually to director of admissions. During that entire time he continued to deliver the programs. In 1993 he returned to high school counseling in a position at Hinsdale South High School that he continues to hold. His seminars continued.

During the past thirty-plus years, the challenges for families have become more significant. After delivering seminars to more than 200,000 families over that time and visiting with well over 2,000 families one on one, Palmasani radically changed his approach in 2008. The challenges of college costs were now so great for families that the solutions would require a new way of looking at the traditional college search and selection process. He developed Financial Fit and began to use technology to deliver the message to a much larger audience.

Palmasani continues to deliver his program, "Conquering the Challenges of College Costs," live to high school parents each year. He also developed a student module, "The Economics of Your College Decision," that high school economics teachers can use and a training program, "Counseling Families about College in These Challenging Economic Times," that he uses to train high school counselors.

He has delivered workshops for the Illinois Association of College Admissions Counseling, the Iowa Association of College Admissions Counseling, the National Association of College Admissions Counseling, the College Board, and regional college organizations in several states. His theories are being used by counselors across the country as they work with students and parents concerned about college costs.

His comprehensive Financial Fit program—which features a forty-five-minute parent video, twenty-one short videos that teach families what to do and when to do it, worksheets and outlines, the College Affordability Calculator™, links to nearly 2,000 colleges' net price calculators, the College Comparison Table, and links to all the important forms—is available at the www.collegecountdown.com bookstore.